TOMORROW

TODAY

TOMORROW Today

LARRY RICHARDS

Though intended for personal reading and profit, this book is part of the Victor Adult Elective Series and therefore is also intended for group study. A Leader's Guide with Victor Multiuse Transparency Masters is available from your local bookstore.

VICTOR BOOKS™

A DIVISION OF SCRIPTURE PRESS PUBLICATIONS INC.
USA CANADA ENGLAND

Scripture quotations are taken from the *Holy Bible, New International Version*, © 1973, 1978, 1984 by the International Bible Society. Used by permission of Zondervan Bible Publishers.

Recommended Dewey Decimal Classification: 236
Suggested Subject Heading: BIBLE—PROPHECIES

Library of Congress Catalog Card Number: 86-60869
ISBN: 0-89693-505-1

C O N T E N T S

God's Voice

DAVID was excited! At last he knew what he could do for the Lord he loved so much! David would build God a temple.

It would be a magnificent thing. David could see it in his imagination. It must tower, higher than other buildings, lit each night with bright flares. The gleaming stones must fit together perfectly, drawing every eye higher and higher, as if to seek the Lord. And there would be gold. Yes, every vessel used in worship would be solid gold!

When David shared this plan with his old friend and advisor, the Prophet Nathan, that prophet approved. "Whatever you have in mind, go ahead and do it" (2 Sam. 7:3). But that night God's Word came to Nathan saying, "No!"

Years later David told the story to Solomon, the son who finally did build the temple that David had dreamed of dedicating to the Lord. "I had it in my heart to build a house for the Name of the Lord my God. But this word of the Lord came to me: 'You have shed much blood and have fought many wars. You are not to build a house for My Name. . . . But you will have a son who will be a man of peace and rest. . . . He is the one who will build a house for My Name'" (1 Chron. 22:7-10).

By Jeremiah's time the kingdom David established had known centuries of trouble. Jeremiah, known as the "weeping prophet" because of the agonizing burden of his ministry, carried a message of certain judgment to his generation. God's people had turned away from the Lord again and again. They had worshiped idols and wealth, perverting the justice demanded in God's Law for personal gain. Despite periodic revivals, the moral and spiritual trend was toward even greater sin.

So when the Babylonian army under Nebuchadnezzar began to devastate Palestine, it was Jeremiah's duty to announce to Israel that the enemy was the hand of God Himself. Jerusalem must surrender, and Israel go willingly into captivity. Only by surrender could even greater bloodshed be avoided.

When this Word of the Lord came to Jeremiah, he spoke out as he was instructed:

> This is what the Lord, the God of Israel, says: "Tell the king of Judah, who sent you to inquire of me '. . . the Babylonians will return and attack this city; they will capture it and burn it down.'
>
> This is what the Lord says: "Do not deceive yourselves, thinking, 'The Babylonians will surely leave us.' They will not! Even if you were to defeat the entire Babylonian army that is attacking you and only wounded men were left in their tents, they would come out and burn this city down" (Jer. 37:6-10).

8

Jeremiah's message wasn't welcome. He was accused of being a traitor, and later the captain of the Jerusalem guard arrested him saying, "You are deserting to the Babylonians" (37:13).

But Jeremiah's warning, and the Word of the Lord he uttered, came true. The city of Jerusalem was captured, the temple treasures carried off to Babylon, and both city and temple were totally destroyed.

The Babylonian captivity was not the end. The Jewish people settled down in Babylon, trying to rebuild their shattered lives. But many continued to yearn for the land God promised to Abraham.

In God's time, a generation later, a few thousand did return. They settled around the ruined city, built homes, and scratched out a living in the now-wild land. Yet no matter how hard they worked, each harvest seemed to leave them worse off than they were the year before.

Then the Word of God came to the Prophet Haggai, and he shouted out words given to him by the Lord Almighty. Israel's troubles persisted "because of My house, which remains a ruin, while each of you is busy with his own house" (Hag. 1:9).

Challenged by the prophet's words, the people put everything else aside and committed themselves to rebuild the temple. And the prophet, again speaking for God, told them to note the day it was finished, for God said, "From this day on I will bless you" (2:19).

It's common for us, when we think of prophets, to focus on their visions of the distant future. You and I like to look ahead too. We try to draw different prophecies together, to develop our own picture of what may happen next as history hurtles on to God's intended end. Sometimes we debate the details. Will Jesus return at the beginning of the Tribulation? Or will it be in the middle, or perhaps after those terrible days foretold in each testament? Yet in our debates about prophetic systems we all too often forget a basic fact.

The primary mission of the Old Testament prophet was not to present a systematic picture of the future. The primary mission of a prophet was to be the voice of God to his own generation and to provide Israel with the guidance needed to continue in God's will.

We see it in Nathan, who warned David that God did not want him to build the temple he so yearned to construct. We see it in Jeremiah, who wept as he told his countrymen that the doom centuries of sin had decreed was about to fall upon them. And we see it in Haggai who urged a responsive new generation to rebuild the fallen temple of their God.

Yes, the ministry of the prophets did involve prediction. But even the predictive words of Scripture, as we will see, carried a vital message for the people of each prophet's day. And those predictive words of Scripture convey vital messages for us in our day as well!

Perhaps we shouldn't study prophecy just to build and defend prophetic systems. Perhaps we should study to hear, as Israel heard, the voice of God speaking in their today.

Why Prophets?
The key passage for understanding the role of Old Testament prophets is found in Deuteronomy chapter 18.

In this book Moses reviews God's Law with an Israel poised at last to take the Promised Land. His words are filled with warnings and instructions on how to live close to the Lord when that land has been taken.

One of his warnings focuses on the occult. The pagans who

lived in Palestine practiced a depraved religion. Religious texts from that era show how closely Palestinian religion was linked with gross immorality and how closely it was linked with magical practices designed to manipulate the gods or to gain supernatural guidance for life's decisions.

God's Word is explicit here. His people are to keep completely away from the occult. Moses announced,

> When you enter the land the Lord your God is giving you, do not learn to imitate the detestable ways of the nations there. Let no one be found among you who sacrifices his son or daughter in the fire, who practices divination or sorcery, interprets omens, engages in witchcraft, or casts spells, or who is a medium or spiritist or who consults the dead. Anyone who does these things is detestable to the Lord (18:9-12).

The occult has always held an attraction for human beings. You and I can understand why. We realize how limited human beings are. Any decision we make involves such terrible risk. We can never look ahead and be sure of the outcome of any of our choices. Should we take a particular job? Should we marry this person, or that one? Should we buy a new car now, or wait? What school should we send young Harry to—the local public school, or that new Christian school across town?

Life is filled with decisions like these, decisions that are important because they affect the course of our lives. Whenever you and I make such a decision, we take a risk. Whatever we decide, we may be wrong. And a wrong decision can be something we'll regret for the rest of our lives.

In view of the fact human beings of every place and time must live with this kind of uncertainty, it's not surprising that so many turn to the occult. Astrology, spiritists, tarot cards,

Ouija boards—even the daily paper's horoscope—seem to offer some hope, however small. Any help from beyond seems better than risking all on our judgment of factors so far beyond human control.

Our God knows how vulnerable we are. And He knows how desperately we need supernatural guidance. But God rules out the occult for Israel, and for you and me. He rules it out because He has something far better in mind. God intends us to receive guidance from Him!

Israel had been given one wonderful source of guidance in the Scriptures that Moses penned. The Word itself would lead Israel away from those actions and choices that would harm, and lead to those choices that would bring blessing. But not every situation could be covered in the written revelation. The day would come when David would want to build God a temple, but Scripture would not tell him what to do. The day would come when Nebuchadnezzar would beseige Jerusalem, and nothing in the Pentateuch would indicate surrender. The day would come when a poverty-stricken remnant would agonize over their troubles. Yet the written Word would not explain that their problems were rooted in disregard for God's house. In these situations, and in many others like them, a special word of guidance from God would be desperately needed.

And so Deuteronomy 18 goes on. God's people must never turn to the occult. But they could look to God. For God committed Himself. When a situation arose in which guidance beyond that already provided in Scripture was needed, God Himself would provide that guidance too. "The Lord your God will raise up for you a prophet" (Deut. 18:15).

The prophet would be God's living spokesman, present among God's people in time of need, to give Israel the Lord's guiding word. "I will put My words in his mouth, and he will tell them everything I command him" (18:18).

The prophets of Israel lived among God's people, and in times of need, when special guidance was required, the prophets functioned as the voice of Israel's living God.

God continues to give us just this kind of special guidance today. But for you and me God's spokesman is the Holy Spirit, who lives within us. We have the written Word of God to give shape and structure to our lives. And, as we face personal decisions and choices not covered in the Bible, we have a peace given by the Spirit of God to mark out our every step as His good will.

Why Prophecy about the Future?

It's a fair question. The prophet served as God's spokesman to his own generation. The prophet's mission was to provide supernatural guidance for the people of his own day. Why then is so much stress laid on predictive prophecy, on those visions of the future captured for us in the Word of God?

First, the predictive aspect of the prophet's ministry had an extremely practical contemporary purpose. Prediction authenticated a prophet as God's spokesman.

Deuteronomy gives several marks by which Israel can recognize a prophet. He is to be a Jew, "from among their brothers" (Deut. 18:18). He is to speak in the name of the Lord, and anyone who claims to be a prophet but "who speaks in the name of other gods, must be put to death" (Deut. 18:20). Whatever one who claims to be a prophet may do to authenticate his claim, if his message involves a call to "follow other gods" and "worship them," that prophet is not to be heard (Deut 13:1-3). No true prophet can violate the written Word of God or contradict truth God has revealed. Contradicting Scripture is decisive evidence that a person is not a prophet sent by the Lord.

But neither of the first two tests is decisive. Old Testament history knows many Israelites who claimed, falsely, to speak in the name of Yahweh.

So another decisive mark is provided. Deuteronomy 18:21-22 explains it this way:

> You may say to yourselves, "How can we know when a message has not been spoken by the Lord?" If what a prophet proclaims in the name of the Lord does not take place or come true, that is a message the Lord has not spoken. That prophet has spoken presumptuously. Do not be afraid of him.

Prediction, then, played a significant role in authenticating a prophet as one who was truly God's spokesperson, as one whose words were to be taken seriously.

An incident from Jeremiah's life illustrates this. Hananiah the son of Azzur boldly announced that Jeremiah's pessimistic message was a lie. "This is what the Lord Almighty, the God of Israel, says," Hananiah said. " 'I will break the yoke of the king of Babylon. Within two years I will bring back to this place [Jerusalem] all the articles of the Lord's house . . . and all the other exiles from Judah who went to Babylon' " (Jer. 28:2-4). Hananiah was a Jew. He spoke in the name of the Lord Almighty, the God of Israel. How were God's people to know if his words or Jeremiah's were to be trusted?

Shortly after, God's Word came to Jeremiah, and that prophet confronted Hananiah in front of the priests and all the people.

14

Listen, Hananiah! The Lord has not sent you, yet you have persuaded this nation to trust in lies. Therefore, this is what the Lord says: "I am about to remove you from the face of the earth. This very year you are going to die, because you have preached rebellion against the Lord" (28:15-16).

Two months later Hananiah was dead, and over half a century would pass before the captives returned to Judah from Babylon.

This is one purpose of predictive prophecy. When the prophets were questioned or challenged, God gave them an authenticating word about the future. When what the prophet foretold happened, Israel knew that he truly was the spokesman, the voice of their God.

But this only explains short-term prophecy. The prophecies that you and I study today picture events foretold many lifetimes before they would be fulfilled. Certainly a prophecy that speaks of an event to happen hundreds or even thousands of years afterward can have no authenticating purpose—or can it?

Well, there is one authenticating purpose. As we'll see in the next chapter, many long-term prophecies of the Word of God *have* been fulfilled, literally and exactly, hundreds of years after they were first uttered. When we look at these prophecies, we gain a deeper appreciation for the written Word of God, and we realize that our Scriptures truly are supernatural in origin. Long-term prophecy does authenticate. It authenticates the Scripture itself!

But there was also a contemporary purpose even in long-term prediction. That purpose was not just to provide an outline of future history. That purpose was to underline truth that was to shape the lives of the prophet's listeners.

So predictive prophecy isn't just about tomorrow. Predictive prophecy is about today! It was about the today of the people of each prophet's time. And predictive prophecy is about our own today as well.

Predictive prophecy is the timeless voice of our living God, speaking to us now, showing us a clearer vision of the future, designed to help us learn to live godly and productive lives.

Tomorrow Today

That's what this book is about. It's about the meaning of the great predictive prophecies of Scripture for you and for me today. Yes, we could look at each prophecy and use it to construct a picture of history's end. Some of the details might be unclear, but the portrait of future history would probably be accurate in its broad sweep and scope. But when we concentrate on such systems, we risk missing something important.

You see, prophecies are not found in Scripture in a systematic way. One prophet records a stunning picture of judgment and describes a great northern army sweeping down on Palestine. Another prophet shares his bright vision of a New Covenant to be made with the house of Israel. Still another prophet outlines events in the centuries destined to pass between the time of Nebuchadnezzar and the appearance of Messiah the Prince. Predictive prophecy in Scripture is like this: one aspect of the future captures a prophet's attention. He shares his vision—and goes on to apply it, showing how that which is coming some distant tomorrow still affects today.

So in this book you and I will go back in Scripture to

explore the situations from which each prophet spoke and to discover the importance of his message for his day. And then we'll go on to see how each prophet's vision of a distant tomorrow is intended to shape our lives, our values, our attitudes, our choices, and our personal relationship with the Lord.

We will look at the prophet's bold visions of tomorrow. And as we gaze ahead, we will pause to see the meaning of God's "tomorrow" for our own "today."

Explore

1. Think for a moment of some of the great predictive prophecies of Scripture that you know. How do you think each was intended to affect the people of the prophet's day? How do you think each is intended to affect Christians today?

2. The author suggests that many people are drawn to the occult because of life's uncertainties. A number of Christians too are attracted to modern seers (like Jeanne Dixon) and are regular readers of newspaper horoscopes. How do you think Deuteronomy 18:9-13 applies to them? To what other modern guidance practices might it apply?

Why do you suppose God is so insistent that believers reject such avenues of guidance?

CHAPTER TWO
Certain and Sure

HIS vision was a dark one. Micah saw nations gathered against his people, and Jerusalem under seige. Israel's current ruler will be killed. But then, suddenly, light bursts through the clouds and Micah writes: "But you, Bethlehem Ephrathah, though you are small among the clans of Judah, out of you will come for me one who will be ruler over Israel, whose origins are from of old, from ancient times" (Micah 5:2). Without a break, Micah's pen moves on, speaking of the abandonment of God's people until this one comes to shepherd God's flock in the strength of the Lord.

The prophet, writing some seven hundred years before Christ, has pinpointed the place of Jesus' birth.

Isaiah, a contemporary of Micah's, also saw far ahead. In chapter 53 of his book Isaiah writes, "He was assigned a grave with the wicked, and with the rich in His death, though He had done no violence, nor was any deceit in His mouth"

(53:9). Seven hundred years before Jesus was hanged between thieves on Calvary's cross and then was placed in the nearby tomb of Joseph of Arimathea, Isaiah accurately described the scene. Jesus was crucified where common criminals were executed; He was buried in the freshly hewn tomb of one of Jerusalem's wealthiest men.

Isaiah had other visions too. In one of them he foresaw a regathering of Israel after a terrible exile from their promised land. Isaiah made the announcement, claiming that it is the Lord

> who says of Jerusalem, "It shall be inhabited," of the towns of Judah, "They shall be built," and of their ruins, "I will restore them" . . . who says of Cyrus, "He is my shepherd and will accomplish all that I please; he will say of Jerusalem, 'Let it be rebuilt,' and of the temple, 'Let its foundations be laid'" (Isa. 44:26, 28).

Some 200 years after Isaiah's prophecy the Babylonian Empire fell to the Medo-Persians. The Persian conqueror reversed the Babylonian policy of removing defeated nations from their homelands and instituted a policy of return. Among his decrees encouraging ethnic groups to resettle their homelands was an edict permitting the Jews to rebuild the Jerusalem temple and ordering that all costs be paid from the Persian treasury.

The name of the ruler who conquered Babylon and issued this decree? Cyrus.

We could multiply examples almost endlessly. Prophecies about Jesus. Prophecies about cities, like Tyre. Prophecies about empires. Prophecies that were fulfilled in history literally hundreds of years after they were made!

There are three important things we can conclude from

what we see of fulfilled prophecy. First, we are assured that God exists and is in full control of history. Isaiah calls on Israel to fix this great truth in mind.

> Remember the former things, those of long ago; I am God, and there is no other; I am God, and there is none like Me. I make known the end from the beginning, from ancient times, what is still to come. I say: "My purpose will stand, and I will do all that I please" (46:9-10).

Only One who is truly God is able to declare with such certainty, "What I have said, that will I bring about; what I have planned, that will I do" (46:11).

Second, fulfilled prophecy gives us great confidence in our Bible. Scripture presents itself as a Word coming from God Himself, filled with truth no person could know otherwise. Peter reminds his readers that "we did not follow cleverly invented stories" (2 Peter 1:16). Indeed, "we have the word of the prophets made more certain" in historic fulfillment of their predictions (1:19). It's clear, as Peter says, that "prophecy never had its origin in the will of man, but men spoke from God as they were carried along by the Holy Spirit" (1:21).

Third, fulfilled prophecy established a pattern. We see that the predictions of the prophets are fulfilled *literally*, in the sense that the historic events that fulfill them are *recognizably* the events the prophets described.

Isaiah, writing of Jesus' death and burial, could not have known beforehand just what his words meant. But now, looking back, we see how accurately and literally he described historic events.

Interpreting Prophecy

It's exciting to see in fulfilled prophecy how trust-worthy Scripture is and to realize how firmly in control God is of history's flow. When current events frighten us and international tensions grow, we Christians can find rest. God is sovereign still, and events are moving toward His intended end. But we shouldn't be too quick to take comfort in our interpretation of what those current events mean or in what we imagine will happen next.

Why not? Why not, if the word of prophecy is so sure?

Simply because it isn't all that easy to interpret prophetic passages before the events they describe happen. And it's even more difficult to fit prophetic events together in a systematic way. You see, there are a few problems.

Problem one: apocalyptic literature. Much biblical prophecy in both testaments focuses on history's end and events associated with it. This literature is filled with language and descriptions that we simply must take as symbolic. The prophet's vision catapults him ahead, and he writes about what he sees. But he is limited in the words he can use in his descriptions.

Just imagine for a moment you are your own great-great-great-grandparent. Suddenly you're catapulted in a vision into the 20th century. In your vision you watch a shuttle hurtle into space and see cars streaming along a superhighway. And then you try to describe what you've seen for people living in 1805! What words will you use? What images can express the things you've seen?

This is just the problem experienced by John on the Isle of Patmos. Suddenly he was catapulted ahead and witnessed events associated with history's end. He described exactly what he saw. But he had to use words and images that came from his own time, words and images like these in Revelation 9:2-6:

> The sun and sky were darkened by the smoke from the Abyss. And out of the smoke locusts came down upon the earth and were given power like that of scorpions of the earth. They were told not to harm the grass of the earth or any plant or tree, but only those people who did not have the seal of God on their foreheads. They were not given power to kill them, but only to torture them for five months. And the agony they suffered was like that of the sting of a scorpion when it strikes a man. During those days men will seek death, but will not find it; they will long to die, but death will elude them.

One day that prophecy will be fulfilled, and fulfilled literally. What happens will be recognizable as what John has described. But until it *does* happen, we'll remain uncertain about just what John's vision really means.

Problem two: time and sequence. It was a courtesy. The village's most famous son, who was making such a name for Himself teaching in Galilee, had returned home. So the ruler of the Nazareth synagogue handed Jesus the scroll of the Prophet Isaiah. Jesus unrolled it, and finding a particular place, He began to read.

> The Spirit of the Lord is on me, because He has anointed me to preach good news to the poor. He has sent me to proclaim freedom for the prisoners and recovery of sight for the blind, to release the oppressed, to proclaim the year of the Lord's favor (Luke 4:18-19).

23

Handing back the scroll, Jesus said, "Today this scripture is fulfilled" (4:21).

What's so fascinating is to turn back to Isaiah 61:1-2, the passage Jesus read. There we discover where Jesus stopped. You see, Isaiah continues on without a break to add "and the day of vengeance of our God!"

We understand why Jesus stopped. Jesus came the first time to die, to make the grace of God available to everyone who will believe. Jesus truly ushered in "the year of the Lord's favor." You and I also know that Jesus will come again. When He does come, it will be "in blazing fire with His powerful angels" to "punish those who do not know God and do not obey the Gospel of our Lord Jesus" (2 Thes. 1:7-8).

Jesus' first coming is associated with release. His second coming is associated with vengeance.

But Isaiah didn't know! Isaiah had no notion that the prophecies he penned described not one but two comings of the Messiah. A two-thousand-year gap lies between words found in a single sentence in a single prophetic verse!

Prophetic passages simply don't pay much attention to such things as time and sequence, so these are particularly hard for us to nail down. Peter even pictures the prophets pouring over their own writings, searching "intently and with the greatest care, trying to find out the time and circumstances to which the Spirit of Christ in them was pointing when He predicted the sufferings of Christ and the glories that would follow" (1 Peter 1:10, 11). The prophets knew something of *what* would happen. But the time and the circumstances—the sequences, the way things all fit together—escaped them.

This is important for you and me to remember when we read books about prophecy that announce with certainty just what is scheduled to happen next or provide month-by-month sequences of events that prophecy assures us do lie ahead. Yes, there are prophecies yet to be fulfilled. Yes, like the prophets of old, you and I may well search them intently, trying to discover times and circumstances. But these are just the things we will *not* know until the prophecy comes to pass.

Problem three: partial and multiple fulfillment. John the Baptist shook his head and denied it. "Are you Elijah?" the Jerusalem delegation asked. "I am not" (John 1:21).

The question was important, because the prophet Malachi had said some 400 years earlier, "I will send you the Prophet Elijah before that great and dreadful Day of the Lord comes" (Mal. 4:5). Israel took prophecy seriously. Was John the promised Elijah?

John said "No." But later when Jesus' disciples asked our Lord about the Elijah prophecy, Jesus explained "Elijah has already come, and they did not recognize him" (Matt. 17:12). And the disciples realized He was talking about John the Baptist.

We've a right to be confused—until we recognize another feature of prophecy. At times things that the prophets foretell have a multiple or a contingent fulfillment. John the Baptist ministered "in the spirit and power of Elijah" (Luke 1:17). If Israel had accepted Jesus as Messiah, John's ministry could have been considered a sufficient fulfillment. But Israel did not. So many students of prophecy are convinced that one of the "two witnesses" whom Revelation associates with history's end is actually Elijah, come in complete fulfillment of Malachi's inspired word.

One other illustration. In Deuteronomy 28 we read that when Israel rejects God, the people will be torn from their land and scattered among the nations (see 28:64-68). In Deuteronomy 30 we find the promise that when future generations return to the Lord, they will be regathered, and the nation reestablished in Palestine (30:1-10). The prophets often repeat each of these themes. And it has already happened! Sinning Israel was torn from its homeland by the Babylonians and was later restored under Cyrus. But prophets who wrote *after* this return still repeat the same themes! And another great scattering took place after Jerusalem was razed by Titus in A.D. 70. Is another great return also destined to take place? Is this happening in modern Israel, reestablished in 1948?

These illustrations do give us some sense of the complexity of prophecy. There is partial fulfillment. Some historic events are considered sufficient to fulfill a prophecy, even though a fuller, complete fulfillment still lies ahead. And there is multiple fulfillment. Some prophecies express themes that are repeated again and again in Israel's history and yet seem to suggest an ultimate fulfillment at history's end.

What Is Ahead?

Scripture's prophetic word is sure and certain. What the Bible says will happen will surely take place. We have God's Word for it, and He retains full control of human history. When fulfillment does come, fulfillment will be literal. We will recognize the events that happen as the events foretold in the Bible. Those Old Testament prophecies that have been fulfilled teach us that fulfillment will be literal.

But looking ahead, we can't be too sure about the details. Prophetic language uses symbols and images that are hard to interpret. Prophetic passages fail to make distinctions about time and sequence. And some prophesied events have partial or multiple fulfillment. So we make a mistake if we fasten with too much confidence on a particular prophetic system or are convinced we know the order of coming events.

Sometimes too much certainty about our interpretation of prophecy can lead to problems. More than one group has stood waiting on some hillside, sure Jesus would return that night. And every one of these groups has stumbled down from the hilltop disappointed, shamefacedly trying to pick up the threads of earthly life once again.

How terrible it would be if a President, convinced that Russia was the Bible's great northern power and that war was inevitable, failed to negotiate for peace!

Or remember the American Christian who planned to bomb the Mosque of Omar, which stands in Jerusalem on the ancient temple site, because he was convinced from prophecy it must be destroyed and a Jewish temple erected before Jesus could return to earth?

In each of these illustrations Christians drew conclusions from *their prophetic systems* and acted on those conclusions. But because of the problems we've looked at, we can't be certain that any of the systems we develop are correct. It's dangerous to base personal or political actions on any system constructed by linking prophesied events together in a timed sequence.

Tomorrow Today

Still, we *are* to base our present actions on prophecy! We *are* to apply what God says about tomorrow in our own todays. How do we know? We know because we see it done in the Bible! Paul describes the Rapture, and says, "Therefore encourage each other with these words" (1 Thes. 4:18). Peter sees the earth itself burst into flames, and says, "Since everything will be destroyed in this way, what kind of people ought you to be?" (2 Peter 3:11) What the Bible does is to apply *prophetic events* to our today—but *not prophetic systems.*

And that's just what we'll do in this study. We won't try to build a system. We will try to view, with the prophets, events that lay beyond their time. And we will see how such events, events that surely will take place, are to shape the lives of God's people in our own today.

Explore

1. Look at these prophetic passages. What interpretative "problems" the author discusses might they involve? Joel 2:28-32, with Acts 2:14-21. Daniel 8:1-12, with 8:19-22. Isaiah 7:3-17, with Matthew 1:22-23.

2. Some Old Testament passages do seem to suggest an overall sequence for events at history's end. Look for instance at Zechariah 12:10–14:21. What are the major events and their sequence? What additional prophesied events are you aware of, and how do you think they fit into the sequence?

CHAPTER THREE
A Tale of Two Cities

THE year is 760 B.C. City One stretches out impressively over a vast plain. Over a day's walk beyond the outskirts of its first suburbs, you can see the massive walls of the central city. It's a proud city, and rightly so. It is the capital of a great empire, destined to grow even greater in the ancient middle eastern world.

The city is Nineveh, home to some 600,000 people. It's the hub of the expansionist Assyrian Empire, a world power rivaled only by Egypt.

City Two lies in a newly resurgent land. After decades of national decline, a war between nearby enemies, which shattered the military power of both, created a power vacuum. Led by a bold, aggressive ruler, Jeroboam II, this recently despised people exploded outward to retake control of lands that had long been lost.

Along with the expanded boundaries came a surge of prosperity. Jeroboam's victories meant that his nation controlled trade routes that linked the nations of the ancient world. Revenues poured in from taxes and duties, and suddenly a land that had been poor became rich!

But the wealth was distributed unequally. The older aristocracy of nobles and priests and the new merchant class that had sprung up kept the wealth for themselves. They demanded luxury goods and residences, and gradually the pattern of the society began to change.

Concentrated wealth merely increased greed. Heavier and heavier taxes were levied on workers, and the wealthy became land-hungry. The rich forced small farmers to sell property which had been in their families for centuries so they could build vast country estates. Many of the poor were forced by hunger to sell themselves and their families into slavery, becoming serfs on land they had once owned.

Even smaller merchants were corrupted and used rigged weights to measure out purchases. The justice system failed as judges took bribes from the rich and joined the oppressors. The middle class began to disappear; the nation was increasingly divided into the very rich and the oppressed poor.

The nation we're describing was Israel, the Northern Kingdom, which in 760 B.C. was approaching the end of the long reign of Jeroboam II. Israel had wealth and power. But the national resurgence had stimulated even greater moral and spiritual decline. Even in City Two, Bethel, where Israel came to worship God.

The First Prophet

Our tale of two cities is also the story of two prophets. The name of the first is Jonah, a very popular figure in Israel in 760 B.C. And no wonder he was popular! After all, it was

Jonah's mission to foretell victory after victory for the kingdom Jeroboam II led!

We read about him in 2 Kings 14:25. There, where the Bible reports on Jeroboam's reign, it says that this king was "the one who restored the boundaries of Israel from Lebo Hamath to the Sea of Arabah, in accordance with the Word of the Lord, the God of Israel, *spoken through His servant Jonah son of Amittai,* the prophet from Gath Hepher" (italics mine).

When Israel had been divided into the Northern and Southern kingdoms (Israel and Judah) after Solomon's death, Jeroboam I had feared that if his Israelites went to Jerusalem to worship God, the nations might be reunited and his kingdom lost. So Jeroboam I set up his own system for worshiping the Lord, counterfeiting the Law's priesthood, its festivals, and its worship center. Bethel and Dan were established as the cities where citizens of the Northern Kingdom should come to worship the God of Abraham, Isaac, and Jacob.

All this was in direct and terrible violation of Scripture. In fact, as in our day citizens flee across the iron curtain to freedom, in that day thousands of Jews deserted the Northern Kingdom to resettle in Judah, where God could be worshiped as the Law ordained. Certainly the disobedience of the new nation Israel merited divine punishment. Why then the prosperity and resurgence of power? Why send the Prophet Jonah to foretell great victories to be won by a disobedient people? Scripture tells us that "the Lord had seen how bitterly everyone in Israel, whether slave or free, was suffering; there was no one to help them. And since the Lord had not said He would blot out the name of Israel from under heaven, He saved them by the hand of Jeroboam" (2 Kings 14:26-27). God cared for Israel, even when His people rejected and disobeyed Him.

So Jonah was a popular prophet. His mission was to foretell military success for his homeland. No wonder he enjoyed the respect and approval of all!

And then God told Jonah to go to Nineveh.

Jonah was to go to Nineveh, and "preach against it, because its wickedness has come up before Me" (Jonah 1:2). We all know the story. Jonah immediately left—to take passage on a ship heading in the opposite direction! God brought a terrible storm, and when the sailors realized Jonah was the cause, the prophet was reluctantly thrown overboard. Swallowed by a great fish which God had prepared, Jonah repented. He would go to Nineveh after all. And he did.

Arriving on the outskirts of the city, Jonah began walking, shouting as he went, "Forty more days and Nineveh will be destroyed" (Jonah 3:4).

And the Ninevites believed God's message! "They declared a fast, and all of them, from the greatest to the least, put on sackcloth" as a symbol of repentance (3:5). In a royal decree the king commanded everyone to "call urgently on God" and "give up their evil ways" (3:8).

Jonah left Nineveh. He stopped at a safe distance and built a shelter there for shade. Then Jonah waited to watch Nineveh be destroyed. When forty days passed and the city still stood, Jonah slipped into angry despair.

It was then Jonah revealed why he'd run away in the first place. "I knew You are a gracious and compassionate God, slow to anger and abounding in love, a God who relents from sending calamity" (4:2). Jonah, the patriotic prophet, had *wanted* God to destroy Nineveh, a potential enemy of his homeland! Jonah had been afraid that if Nineveh were warned, the people would repent—just as they had. And Jonah was afraid that God, so gracious and compassionate and loving, would relent—just as He had.

The Second Prophet

It's still about 760 B.C., and another man is about to be sent by God on a prophetic mission. This man's name is Amos. He's not a prophet or even a seminarian—that is, a "prophet's son" (Amos 7:14). Amos works as a shepherd and also tends sycamore trees, whose fruit feeds animals and is sold for the tiniest of coins as food for the poor. He lives in Judah, neighbor to hostile Israel. Like Jonah, Amos is about to be sent by God to a foreign land (Israel), with a message of coming judgment.

There are a number of parallels between the men and their missions. Each is to go alone to a foreign country, carrying a message of doom. Each is to go to a land where he will be unknown, where no credentials have established him as God's spokesman. Each mission is dangerous, for there's no reason to expect the confronted peoples to welcome the prophet's charge of wickedness or warning of wrath!

When Amos obediently crosses the border into Israel, we can expect that he felt uncertain and more than a little fearful. Being a prophet was new to him! But Amos went. We can imagine him, dressed in the simple garments of the poor man he is, entering Bethel and walking past rows of newly constructed luxury homes. We can imagine him walking through the market, where the poor were sold in stalls that stood next to shops featuring the latest in footwear and imported sofas for the rich.

We can sense Amos' tension as he comes near the newly beautified worship center, takes a deep breath, and begins to shout out his message to the rich and powerful.

Amos' preaching began with a proclamation of judgment to come on all the surrounding nations. For the sins of these people, God announces, "I will not turn back my wrath" (Amos 1:3, 6, 11, 13; 2:1, 4). But then Amos focuses on his hearers and in a loud, bold voice shouts out the message that God has told him to deliver.

> For three sins of Israel, even for four, I will not turn back my wrath. They sell the righteous for silver, and the needy for a pair of sandals. They trample on the heads of the poor as upon the dust of the ground and deny justice to the oppressed. Father and son use the same girl and so profain my holy name. They lie down beside every altar on garments taken in pledge. In the house of their God they drink wine taken as fines.... Now then, I will crush you as a cart crushes when loaded with grain. The swift will not escape, the strong will not muster their strength, and the warrior will not save his life (2:6-8, 13).

But Amos' mission was not completed with this single warning. He preached other sermons during the brief days he was in Israel, sermons that explained the basis for God's warning of judgment and at the same time offered hope.

> You hate the one who reproves in court and despise him who tells the truth. You trample on the poor and force him to give you grain. Therefore, though you have built stone mansions, you will not live in them; though you have planted lush vineyards, you will not drink their wine. For I know how many are your offenses and how great your sins. You oppress the righteous and take bribes and you deprive the poor of justice in your courts. Therefore the prudent man keeps quiet in such

34

times, for the times are evil (5:10-13).

And, with the confrontation and warning came a message of hope. "Seek good, not evil, that you may live. Then the Lord God Almighty will be with you, just as you say He is. Hate evil, love good; maintain justice in the courts. *Perhaps the Lord God Almighty will have mercy on the remnant of Joseph* (5:14-15, italics mine).

Two Cities, One Message

Jonah and Amos were each sent, alone and without a prophet's usual authenticating signs, to foreign lands. Jonah went to pagan Nineveh, Amos to a Bethel where the people of Israel gathered to worship Jehovah, their forefather Abraham's God.

Jonah preached a simple message of imminent judgment: in forty days Nineveh will be destroyed. The people of Nineveh looked beyond the appearance to hear not some ragged foreigner but the very voice of God. Nineveh repented, called urgently on God, and gave up "their evil ways and their violence" (Jonah 3:8). There was no need for Jonah to detail their sins; their own consciences convicted them.

But they did repent. And God, ever compassionate and loving, "did not bring upon them the destruction He had threatened" (3:10).

What an object lesson for Israel! Surely God, who refused to destroy pagan Nineveh, would withhold judgment on His own covenant people Israel, if only they too would repent!

But Israel did not repent! Amos' first sermon, which like Jonah's announced coming judgment, did not provoke a response. Perhaps the people looked at Amos' clothes and dismisssed him as just one of the rabble-rousing poor. Perhaps he was resented as a foreigner, a citizen of Judah, whose people think their religion is better than Israel's. Perhaps the Israelites had religious objections: what predictions had Amos made to authenticate his message?

So Amos' later sermons become more specific. He detailed the violations of God's Law. He condemned their indifference to the poor. Amos even offered what Jonah never did—the promise that God would relent if only Israel would repent.

Pagan Assyria recognized the voice of God and responded wholeheartedly to Him. God's own people, Israel, shut their ears tight so they would not hear, and refused to respond to the prophet whom God had sent.

And in 722 B.C. Sargon II of Assyria, whose capital city was Nineveh, totally crushed Israel. Her capital city, Samaria, was razed, and the worship centers at Bethel and Dan were destroyed. The surviving population of the Northern Kingdom was taken out of that land into a captivity from which they never returned.

Tomorrow Today

In 760 B.C. two prophets were sent on missions for God.

Each foretold divine judgment. The people of Nineveh believed, responded, and were spared. The very survival of Nineveh served as an object lesson to Israel. If only Israel, however great her sins, would turn to the Lord and keep His great and good Law, Israel too would have hope.

Hope for today glows in the message of these ancient prophets, and warnings flash. Each of us, and our society, needs to acknowledge God as a moral judge, who will punish sin found in individuals and nations. But we see hope in God's compassion and love. It's not too late for us yet. Repentance and a return to righteousness promise judgment's stay.

Explore

1. Can you discover a principle here that might create additional problems in interpreting prophecy?

2. What do you think a modern Amos would be most likely to condemn in our society? In our churches?

3. How well do you think Jonah understood God? (See 4:1-2). How well do you think Jonah understood himself? (See 4:3-11). Why do you suppose some who understand God quite well fail to share the Lord's attitudes toward others?

4. If you were to personally choose one thing to do in response to what you've discovered in Jonah and Amos, what would that one thing be?

CHAPTER FOUR
Hope and a Future

FOR some forty years now Jeremiah had warned the people of Judah. They'd mocked his tears and laughed at his warning of judgment. Now, in this tenth year of Zedekiah king of Judah, the eighteenth year of Nebuchadnezzar of Babylon—a year that we identify as 588 B.C.—the terror had come.

Jeremiah, confined in the royal guards' quarters, could hear the shouts and hear the rumbling of the great siege engines that even now threatened the mighty walls of Jerusalem. Thousands of the Babylonians were building dirt ramps. Other thousands fed fires, burning in protected pits dug against the base of the wall, intended to weaken the great stones. Other hundreds fired arrows from mobile towers, while hundreds more manned catapults.

Beyond this first ring of attackers a vast army stretched out over the devastated land. The rest of Judah was gone. Its few walled cities were crushed, its trees cut down for fuel, its fertile fields trampled flat by the ruthless Babylonian hordes. Everything Jeremiah had prophesied was coming true, now.

Jeremiah crouched in his corner of the courtyard, isolated there so his pessimism couldn't destroy the defenders' morale. Jeremiah had boldly confronted his worried king and told him, "If you fight against the Babylonians, you will not succeed" (Jer. 32:5). Zedekiah couldn't have a man who talked like that wandering free!

But now a very personal word from God came suddenly to the aging prophet. "Hanamel son of Shallum your uncle is going to come to you and say, 'Buy my field at Anathoth, because as nearest relative it is your right and duty to buy it'" (32:6). Anathoth, Jeremiah's birthplace, was in occupied territory; the field of his cousin was now trampled and worthless. Still, God wanted Jeremiah to purchase that field. So when Hanamel came, Jeremiah did as God wished.

> I bought the field at Anathoth from my cousin Hanamel and weighed out for him seventeen shekels of silver. I signed and sealed the deed, and had it witnessed, and weighed out the silver on the scales. I took the deed of purchase—the sealed copy containing the terms and conditions, as well as the unsealed copy—and I gave this deed to Baruch son of Neriah, the son of Mahseiah, in the presence of my cousin Hanamel and of the witnesses who had signed the deed and of all the Jews sitting in the courtyard of the guard. In their presence I gave Baruch these instructions: "This is what the Lord Almighty, the God of Israel says, 'Take these documents . . . and put them in a clay jar so they will last a long time'" (32:9-14).

40

A Puzzled Prayer

When it was over Jeremiah turned immediately to God. The prophet acknowledged God as Sovereign Lord (32:17-22) and then posed his question. This people "did not obey You or follow Your law; they did not do what You commanded them to do. So You brought all this disaster upon them. See how the siege ramps are built up to take the city. Because of the sword, famine and plague, the city will be handed over to the Babylonians who are attacking it. What You said has happened, as You now see. And though the city will be handed over to the Babylonians, You, O Sovereign Lord, say to me, 'Buy the field with silver and have the transaction witnessed'" (32:23-25).

The obvious question is, Why? Why would God command the prophet to buy a worthless field in a land dedicated to destruction?

It was a good question. When certain disaster has come, what future can there be? Even the most optimistic of Jerusalem's defenders must have known in his heart that the situation was hopeless. And he must have recognized the rightness of God's judgment. And when disaster comes, even a person who doesn't see his troubles as punishment is robbed of hope.

The local plant shuts down and the breadwinner's job is lost; suddenly even the home you've worked for becomes worthless. You make a bad choice, or a bad move, and lose everything you've saved. Your fiancé unexpectedly breaks the engagement. A life-threatening illness strikes one of your loved ones. There are so many disasters we're vulnerable to, even when what happens isn't a judgment from God. How difficult at such times to maintain a positive attitude or to hope!

Hope seemed impossible to Jeremiah. The siege ramps

almost topped Jerusalem's walls. Famine and plague had weakened the defenders. The once-fertile fields of Palestine were hardened, dusty, and dead. And despite all this, God told His prophet to buy a field.

He Should Have Known
If anyone should have had hope that dark day it was Jeremiah. Jeremiah had prophesied the disaster. But Jeremiah also had delivered other messages from God. In particular, some seventeen years earlier Jeremiah had delivered one very unusual message. It had started off like one of his typical warnings.

"Turn now, each of you, from your evil ways and your evil practices" Jeremiah had shouted (25:5). But Jeremiah had been saying things like this for twenty-three years, as had the prophets before him, and no one had listened. No one paid attention then, even when Jeremiah announced in the name of the Lord Almighty, "I will summon all the peoples of the north and my servant Nebuchadnezzar king of Babylon...and I will bring them against this land and its inhabitants....I will completely destroy them and make them an object of horror" (25:8-9).

But then Jeremiah's message had taken an unusual turn. Nestled among the words of judgment had been a promise intended to comfort and awaken hope!

> This whole country will become a desolate wasteland, and these nations will serve the king of Babylon seventy years.
>
> But when the seventy years are fulfilled, I will punish the king of Babylon and his nation, the land of the

42

Babylonians, for their guilt, declares the Lord, and will make it desolate forever (25:11-12).

The Babylonians would triumph in Jeremiah's day, *but not forever.* Judah and the other nations of the Middle East would serve Babylon, *but only for seventy years!*

This was the thing that Jeremiah had forgotten, the thing that had been forced from his mind by the overwhelming pain of Judah's immediate disaster. But God had not forgotten. And when Jeremiah prayed, God explained His purpose again to His troubled servant.

The Jerusalem Jeremiah knew would surely be destroyed "by the sword, famine and plague" (32:36). The city and its people would be handed over to the king of Babylon, just as Jeremiah had prophesied. But this was not to be the end! God's love outlasts His anger.

> I will surely gather them from all the lands where I banished them in my furious anger and great wrath; I will bring them back to this place and let them live in safety. They will be My people, and I will be their God. . . . I will never stop doing good to them, and I will inspire them to fear Me, so that they will never turn away from Me. I will rejoice in doing them good and will assuredly plant them in this land with all My heart and soul" (32:37-41).

The Captivity

Looking back in history, we can see that what seemed so dreadful to Jeremiah and his contemporaries was used by God for good. The seventy years the Jewish people spent in Babylon had a purging effect. The deportation took place in

43

three stages: in 605 B.C., in 597 B.C., and in 586 B.C. after the city was destroyed.

Life was not hard for the captives: they lived in Babylon's suburbs as *mushkenu*, free men of lower class, rather than as *wardu*, slaves. Many owned homes or businesses and raised garden crops on fertile, irrigated lands. The Jewish community even retained a degree of self-government. Yet the people yearned for their homeland. And they became sensitive to what they had done as well as to what they had lost.

From the time of the Exodus the Jewish people had proven susceptible to idol worship. Over and over this sin had entrapped them, leading them away from full dedication to the Lord. After the Captivity idolatry was no longer attractive. Later attempts to force the nation to worship idols were even resisted to the death!

The Captivity was also the source of a new institution, the synagogue. Earlier religious life had centered in the temple whose priesthood seldom paid attention to its task of teaching Israel God's Law. Now the captives met in smaller gatherings, not only to worship but to study the written Word. Study of the Old Testament began to take precedence over worship ritual, and a passion for the Word of God would characterize Israel to and beyond Jesus' time.

The disaster that had seemed to be the end of everything to Jeremiah and to the people of his time proved instead to mark a new beginning. And when the seventy years Jeremiah foretold had passed, Babylon fell, and the Persian ruler of the new empire issued his command. Those Jews who wished to return to Palestine could go home.

And what of Babylon? Just as Jeremiah had foretold, that city fell into ruins. Today you can visit the desolate countryside where Babylon stood and see empty mounds scoured by blowing sands. The desert owls and foxes live there, with the rats and mice that are their scurrying prey. But no voice is raised. No children laugh where Nebuchadnezzar erected his Hanging Gardens. No human sound is heard where once great state buildings housed a bureaucracy that issued the decrees that once governed nearly a tenth of our globe.

Again, as always, the prophetic word had come completely true.

As all the prophets had warned, judgment came and Judah was torn from her land. As Jeremiah had foretold, the Captivity lasted just seventy years, and a purified people did return. And as Jeremiah also preannounced, Babylon has been made "desolate forever" (25:12).

Tomorrow Today

But let's return to Jeremiah, as he huddles in the open courtyard next to the barracks of the royal guard. Let's listen with him to the sounds of battle, the shouts and the cries of anguish as Babylon's overwhelming forces surge against a doomed Jerusalem's walls.

How we feel with him! How we sense his anguish, tremble with his fear, weep with him in his pain at the deaths of those he loves.

We can feel with Jeremiah because too often we face tragedies of our own. We experience our own losses, face our own disasters, bear our own scarring pain. When tragedies crush us, we have as much difficulty as Jeremiah in remembering words that might bring us hope.

So we shouldn't be surprised or critical that in the overwhelming presence of tragedy, Jeremiah forgot God's promise that the exile would be limited to seventy years.

It was then God sent cousin Hanamel to sell Jeremiah a worthless field and then that God told Jeremiah to buy. The Prophet Jeremiah was to undertake an act of faith. In the now-desolate land, Jeremiah was to demonstrate by his act a conviction that "fields will be bought for silver, and deeds will be signed, sealed and witnessed in the territory of Benjamin, in the villages around Jerusalem, in the towns of Judah and in the towns of the hill country . . . because I will restore their fortunes, declares the Lord" (32:44).

In the midst of his tragedy God's prophet was to live and act in hope.

And so too are we.

Just as Jeremiah was to look beyond his present experience, you and I are to look beyond our today and realize that, in this world as in the next, our God is committed to acting for our good. Jeremiah knew the time of suffering would end: he had God's Word for that. But we know something Jeremiah could not know. In the crucible of suffering God would purify His people and forge in them a deeper, stronger faith. The idols that tempted the Jewish people would never tempt them again, and the eyes and hearts of Israel would be turned firmly toward God's written Word.

We don't know, when suffering strikes you and me, just what good God intends. But we do know that even in tragedy we can live and act in hope. God's words through Jeremiah, addressed to the Israel of his day, are confirmed to you and me today, for God loves us just as deeply in Jesus Christ: "When seventy years are completed for Babylon, I will come to you and fulfill my gracious promise to bring you back to this place. For I know the plans I have for you, declares the Lord, plans to prosper you and not to harm you, plans to give you hope and a future" (29:10-11).

Explore

1. What experiences have you had in which you felt as Jeremiah must have?

2. What promises of God have given you hope in such times? How did your actions demonstrate hope?

3. What seems to be God's most important message to *you* in this prophecy of Jeremiah? Here are some of the messages, but add any other messages you may have seen: God supervises the depth and extent of our tragedies. God's promises help us live and act in hope despite tragedies. God will bring unexpected good out of our difficult times. God intends good even when He punishes us.

CHAPTER FIVE

On the Heights

EVENING was falling as Habakkuk trudged up toward the hills ranging between Jerusalem and the ruins of Samaria.

Habakkuk should have been happy. At least, a casual observer would think so. This man whom we know simply as "the prophet" (Hab. 1:1) lived during a time of religious reform, in the days of Josiah, King of Judah (639-609 B.C.).

Josiah's grandfather, the evil Manasseh, had destroyed all the copies of the Scriptures he could locate. Josiah, who experienced a personal conversion at age 16 (see 2 Chron. 34:3) and at 20 began to purge Judah of idolatry, had found a copy of the lost Law while repairing the temple. Guided by the Scriptures, Josiah set about his reformation with fresh zeal. He called the Levites back to the ancient temple service, and led his people in a ceremony of renewed commitment to their covenant with God.

But as Habakkuk trudged on, away from Jerusalem and the restored temple, he was a deeply troubled man. The religious reformation was exciting, but superficial. The violence and injustice so deeply ingrained in Judah's national life remained, unchanged.

The sensitive Habakkuk, deeply aware of the holiness of Judah's God, had cried out to Him, describing the moral conditions and asking

> Why do You tolerate wrong? Destruction and violence are before me; there is strife, and conflict abounds. Therefore the law is paralyzed, and justice never prevails. The wicked hem in the righteous, so that justice is perverted (Hab. 1:3-4).

God's people once again knew the Law. But the Mosaic code was not administered by the King or any national police force. Justice depended on the honesty of local elders and the integrity of the witnesses to matters in dispute. In Judah the wicked were so numerous they hemmed in the righteous; with bribes and lies they perverted justice.

And Habakkuk cried out, "How long?" How long could God watch His people torn by violence and destruction, by strife and conflict, and not act?

God had answered Habakkuk. He revealed that He was "going to do something in your days that you would not believe, even if you were told" (1:5). Far to the north, the mighty Assyrian empire was about to fall. Suddenly, unexpectedly, a fierce people whose only trust was in military might was about to crush Assyria and become the dominant world power. Those people were the Babylonians, led by their great conqueror Nebuchadnezzar. Habakkuk, forewarned of their unexpected rise, realized that Babylon was to be the instrument used by God to purge His own people and punish them for their persistent sins.

Habakkuk understood this and accepted it. "We will not die," he had thought. "You have ordained them to punish" (1:12). God's ancient people and God's promises would be preserved through this interlude of discipline.

But then the sensitive Habakkuk suddenly realized that he was faced with a moral quandry. God would use the Babylonians to punish wicked Israel, but the Babylonians were more wicked still! How could God, whose "eyes are too pure to look on evil" and who "cannot tolerate wrong" tolerate using the wicked to swallow up those more righteous than they? (1:13) Besides, the very military successes of the Babylonians would lead them to ridicule God and to worship their own power rather than the Lord of the universe!

And so Habakkuk was on his way up into the mountains. He was on his way to search out, alone, God's answer to the complaint that troubled him so deeply.

Each of us can, or should, share the prophet's concern. We too live in an imperfect world, a world marred like Habakkuk's by injustice and violence. Our society, even though we are known as a "Christian nation," tolerates evils that tear at the heart of our loving God. Those of us who take Scripture seriously realize that judgment lies ahead for us, as it lay ahead for Judah. We do not know God's instrument or God's time. But we know that no nation, no people, exists forever. When evils are tolerated—the denial of the sanctity of human life, the perversion of sex, disregard for the poor and oppressed—that society must and will fall. And even if we are not convinced that Western society deserves divine judgment, we know from prophecy that a terrible time of worldwide war and suffering will surely come.

And yet when a nation is crushed in judgment, the good suffer along with the wicked. And all too often in history victorious powers are, like the Babylonians of Habakkuk's day, more evil than those they overwhelm.

So Habakkuk's quest is one that you and I might well share. The vision of judgment coming tomorrow troubled Habakkuk's today—as it should trouble us today. The prophetic word warns us that for our world too times of tribulation and anguish lie ahead.

The Victors Are Victims

Habakkuk paused at last, standing on one of those high rocky points that had been used in earlier times as watchtowers for early warning against invasions from Judah's northern neighbor. There Habakkuk received an answer that resolved his moral quandary, and with it a stunning vision of the personal price the individual believer must pay when judgment is visited on his nation.

The moral quandary is easily resolved. God simply points out to Habakkuk that the victors are just as much victims of their success as the vanquished! No oppressor, however "successful" he or she seems to be, escapes the *present* judgment of God, to say nothing of the judgment to come! Chapter 2 of Habakkuk's book carefully reports principles of present judgment which God revealed to His troubled prophet and to us.

Hungers cannot be satisfied (2:2-5). God tells Habakkuk that desires that are not upright can never be satisfied. In fact, the very success of the wicked betrays them; they get, but they are never at rest and like death, cannot be satisfied. Always such persons must have more; always they burn for what they do not yet have. No matter how many the successes of such a person, no matter how much he has, these only feed the flames of his desire and never satisfy him.

The principle operates today just as in Habakkuk's time. People look with envy at a popular star, or a multimillionaire. If only we could look inside them, we would discover that where their "success" was driven by unrighteous desires, those desires still burn. Success has brought neither satisfaction, popularity, nor peace. No, don't envy the winner. The victor is a victim too, betrayed by his own raging desires.

Enemies are being created (2:6-8). Everyone who "piles up stolen goods" or "makes himself wealthy by extortion" does so by violating the rights of others. When a person harms others, he creates enemies, and one day such "debtors" will "suddenly arise." The person who does violence creates the very conditions that guarantee he will suffer violence in return.

Material prosperity cannot last (2:9-14). Those in the grip of unrighteous desires yearn for things that cannot last. One person "builds his realm by unjust gain," another defrauds, all to build material security for himself. Such "labor is only fuel for the fire." God has determined that "the earth will be filled with the knowledge of the glory of the Lord, as the waters cover the sea." It is not the material things men struggle for which last. The only solid reality on which to build one's life is God.

God will intervene to punish (2:15-17). The person or people who misuse others will be overwhelmed by destruction; the conquering nation will be conquered. "The cup from the Lord's right hand is coming around to you."

What men trust in will prove useless (2:18-20). The idols in which the wicked trust will be unable to help them when their own turn comes. Whether they are idols of wood and stone or the idols of military power and wealth, such things are lifeless and worthless. It is God who is in His holy temple. It is God who pronounces judgment. All the earth must fall silent, hushed before Him.

So there really is no moral quandary after all. The wicked don't "get away with" their sins. The successful aren't to be envied, or the popular praised and admired. The victors are as much their own victims as those they oppress. How terrible, with all that wealth and power, to be empty and unsatisfied within. How terrible to look at others and fear them as enemies. How terrible to seek security in material things and safety in idols. How terrible for the Babylonians—and how terrible for those who are trapped by their own sinful passions today. We who are the victims of others suffer, yes. But the victors are far worse off than we!

The Innocent Suffer Too

God's unexpected answer satisfied Habakkuk. The moral quandary is resolved; God is at work executing judgment on the victors, even at those moments of their greatest success. And so Habakkuk responds with praise—and a request.

> Lord, I have heard of Your fame; I stand in awe of Your deeds, O Lord. Renew them in our day, in our time make them known; in wrath remember mercy (3:2).

"Lord," Habakkuk prayed, "bring on Your judgment day! In our time make Your deeds known!"

Like some today, Habakkuk was eager for God's purifying judgment to come soon. Judgment would mean suffering for his people. But Habakkuk was eager for God to act.

And then God gave Habakkuk another, terrifying revelation. God showed Habakkuk what it means to live in the day judgment comes.

In a vision, God takes Habakkuk back to the time of the Exodus (Hab. 3:3-7). He sees the glory of God, bright as a white-hot flame, following Israel along the path from Sinai. Habakkuk is shown Israel, sinning on the plains of Midian (cf. Num. 25), and senses the awesome spiritual forces unleashed when that generation is judged for its idolatry and sin. It is as though the ancient mountains crumble, as though the brightness of God's holiness burns so bright that everything it touches writhes in the grip of pestilence or plague. The companions of judgment are anguish, terror, a crushing emotional distress that is unrelieved even by the prospect of death.

Habakkuk is then transported in his vision to another day of judgment (3:8-10). He sees the earth itself shake and quiver as God unleashes the waters of the Genesis Flood. It is as if God were striking the earth with arrow after arrow from His bow, a sight so terrifying that "the mountains saw You and writhed."

Then came yet another vision (3:11-15). This time Habakkuk is shown God, striding across the land, flushed with anger, about to act to deliver His people. The gloating warriors of the enemy, who stormed out to scatter Israel, were themselves scattered in the Red Sea, churned in the waters of divine judgment.

And suddenly Habakkuk realizes that the day of judgment is not something to pray for lightly! The visions God has given have not only taken the prophet back to the events of earlier times. They have shown him the awesome spiritual forces unleashed when God acts in man's world. Awed by his vision, aware now that a visitation by God is enough to make mountains crumble and writhe, Habakkuk at last is afraid.

Habakkuk has gone beyond his intellectual concern with the morality of God to feel personal fear. Habakkuk has at last realized the anguish and pain that even the innocent must suffer when judgment days come.

> I heard and my heart pounded, my lips quivered at the sound; decay crept into my bones, and my legs trembled (3:16).

You know, you and I live in a day when many expect God to act soon, to begin the process that leads to final judgment. They may well be correct. But even if centuries rather than years separate our time from the return of Jesus, we must still live under the threat of judgment. We are vulnerable to war and not safe from natural disasters. Many in our world are experiencing just these things at this moment, and we are not immune. History agrees: societies that countenance sin suffer judgment. The judgment of God may well fall on our country in our time. And then even the innocent will suffer and may die.

This is what Habakkuk saw. This is what silenced his glib request for God to hasten His judgment day. And yet, Habakkuk also saw the secret of inner peace.

> Though the fig tree does not bud and there are no grapes on the vines, though the olive crop fails and the fields produce no food, though there are no sheep in the pen and no cattle in the stalls, yet I will rejoice in the Lord, I will be joyful in God my Saviour (3:17-18).

Whatever happened, and however great the material loss, no one could rob Habakkuk of joy in God his Saviour.

Glancing up then Habakkuk saw a deer, moving quickly and surefootedly on the mountain heights. A misstep would mean death on the rocks far below. But the deer moved confidently, calm and sure. And then Habakkuk realized that he had discovered the greatest truth of all.

> The Sovereign Lord is my strength; He makes my feet like the feet of a deer, He enables me to go on the heights (3:19).

Tomorrow Today

Like Habakkuk, you and I live in an imperfect society. While thankful for the freedoms of our land, we can't help but wonder—what is God's attitude toward a nation that legalizes the murder of unborn human beings? What is His view of pornography, so flippantly dismissed by the majority as "adult"? How does God justify His silence in view of increasing reports of child abuse? How does the Lord feel about a society that refuses to deal with drunk driving and a government that supports the slow murder of its citizens by subsidizing the tobacco industry?

We, like the Judah of Habakkuk's day, may experience a religious revival. But the same kinds of injustices that so disturbed God's sensitive prophet do exist in modern America!

When you and I are disturbed by sins and injustice around us, the ancient words of Habakkuk are reassuring. We need never again wonder why God does not act. As we listen to Habakkuk's message, we realize that no one truly profits from sin. God is acting to exact an inner price now—and judgment lies ahead.

Some Christians, aware that no civilization lasts for all time, have wondered if America's time of judgment may not be near. Yes, thre are signs of growing moral decay. Does this mean that our nation, like Habakkuk's Judah, is rushing toward judgment?

This is something we cannot know. But even if national judgment does lie ahead, you and I can find comfort in Habakkuk's final words. Disasters may await us. Our cities may burn; our economy crumble. Death and destruction may stalk the land. But not even this will be able to rob us of our joy in God or of our confidence that, whatever may come, the Sovereign Lord will be our strength.

He will enable us too "to go on the heights."

Explore

1. Do you see other things in our society or in biblical prophecy that suggest our generation may experience God's judgment on our country or our world? What are some of these things?

2. Should Christians pray for God to judge the sins of our day, or not? Why?

3. Have you experienced any of the principles of present judgment that Habakkuk 2 explains, or seen them at work in the life of anyone you know? Describe briefly.

4. Has God given you joy in and brought you safely through times of great trouble? What did you learn about the Lord from those experiences? How did they affect your values—your view of what is really important in life?

CHAPTER SIX
Not Yet

THE judgment day that Habakkuk foresaw came. Jeremiah lived through the siege of Jerusalem and witnessed the burning of the temple that he and all the godly loved. But many of the Jewish people did not witness it. They were gone, deported to Babylon during earlier invasions.

One of those taken in the first deportation, in 605 B.C., was a teenager named Daniel. He was enrolled with three companions in the King's School, where youths from conquered provinces were trained to become administrators of Nebuchadnezzar's vast, multitongued empire.

Stories of Daniel are among the most familiar in our Bible. We learned them as children—the stories of Daniel in the lions' den, of Daniel interpreting Nebuchadnezzar's dream. And the prophecies of Daniel have become the focus of intense study, for they bring us suddenly to the New Testament age and point us to a time beyond our own when the last chapter in earth's history will be penned.

The most unusual feature of Daniel's prophecy is that, alone among prophetic writings, he provides a careful, detailed time frame within which the prophecies are to be fulfilled. It is this time frame that should have been most significant and comforting to Israel and that continues to have a "today" significance for you and me.

The Times of the Gentiles

Daniel lived in a day when the Jewish homeland was dominated by Babylon, a Gentile (non-Jewish) world power. His prophecies describe political events in the wider world, events that affected a Palestine destined to remain subject to one pagan power after another.

Daniel's political visions and prophecies are found in chapters 2, 7, and 8 of his book. Although the visions differ, each concerns political powers that were to arise between the time of Daniel and the time of history's end. These visions, and the world powers they represent, are shown on the chart found on page 61.

A review of history helps us sense the stunning accuracy of Daniel's prophecies—an accuracy so overpowering that those who deny the supernatural insist the Book of Daniel must have been written hundreds of years after Daniel lived.

Babylon. Under Nebuchadnezzar, Babylon (the head of gold of Daniel 2, and lion of Daniel 7) became the unquestioned ruler of vast territories. Nebuchadnezzar died in 562 B.C. and was succeeded by weaker rulers, and the city of Babylon with its empire was taken by the Medes and Persians in 538 B.C.

Daniel 2, 7, 8

	Babylon (605–538 B.C.)	Medo-Persia (538–331 B.C.)	Greece (331–146 B.C.)	Rome (146 B.C.–A.D. 476)
Daniel 2:31–45 Dream image (603 B.C.)	Head of gold (2:32, 37–38)	Breast, arms of silver (2:32, 39)	Belly, thighs of brass (2:32, 39)	Legs of iron Feet of iron and clay (2:33, 40–41)
Daniel 7 First vision: Four Beasts (553 B.C.)	Lion (7:4)	Bear (7:5)	Leopard (7:6)	Strong Beast (7:7, 11, 19, 23)
Daniel 8 Second vision: Ram and goat (551 B.C.)		Ram (8:3–4, 20)	Goat with one horn (8:5–8, 21) Four horns (8:8, 22) Little horn (8:9–14)	

Medo-Persia. Cyrus was a great and humanitarian ruler. He reorganized the administration of the Babylonian Empire and restored captive peoples to their homelands. Under this new policy, the Jews were freed to resettle Palestine and were even given treasury funds to finance the rebuilding of their temple.

The Medo-Persian empire (the breast and arms of silver of Daniel 2, the bear of chapter 7, and the ram of chapter 8) grew to include even Egypt. For a time it seemed likely to overwhelm Europe as well. But several Persian invasions were thrown back by the Greeks. Internal revolts and a weakening of central authority led to the empire's collapse some two centuries after Cyrus.

Greece. The Persian invasion convinced the Greek city states that they must end the Eastern menace. But it was not until 334 B.C. that Alexander the Great of Macedon led outnumbered forces into empire lands. By 331 he had conquered the empire, and he ruled! But Alexander died young, in 323 B.C., and his empire was divided among four of his generals. All this was foretold by Daniel, especially in his vision of a goat with one horn to be succeeded by four horns (8:5-22).

Rome. The final world power with which Daniel deals is Rome (the iron legs and feet of Daniel 2, the strong beast of Daniel 7). It was Rome that gradually took over the territories of the old Eastern Empire and welded them with its own European holdings to become the mightiest of the world powers.

But how do we know that the images in Daniel's visions really do represent these historic nations?

We know because the Book of Daniel explains his visions. Look, and see history revealed before its time, by an angel who interpreted Daniel's visions to the prophet.

> I am going to tell you what will happen later in the time
> of wrath, because the vision concerns the appointed
> time of the end. The two-horned ram that you saw
> represents the kings of Media and Persia. The shaggy
> goat is the king of Greece, and the large horn between
> his eyes is the first king. The four horns that replaced
> the one that was broken off represent four kingdoms
> that will emerge from his nation but will not have the
> same power (8:19-22).

The explanation continues. But the prophecy is explained,
and its complete accuracy is witnessed to by the history of
those lands.

God told Daniel, and through him the Jewish people, what
was to happen in the coming centuries. God revealed a long
tomorrow, to have a distinct impact on Israel's today.

The Times and Seasons

But most stunning in Daniel's prophecies is the detailed
information about time.

In Daniel 9 Daniel is told, "Seventy 'sevens' are decreed for
your people and your holy city to finish transgression, to put
an end to sin, to atone for wickedness, to bring in everlasting
righteousness, to seal up vision and prophecy and to anoint
the most holy" (9:24).

The seventy 'sevens' are seventy clusters of seven years
each. In a 490-year span, during which history will traverse its
ordained course and empire follow empire, God's purposes
will be complete, and history reach its end.

But the world did not end 490 years after Daniel wrote! Our
era had hardly begun! How can we explain *that?* But Daniel
goes on. The 490 years are divided into three groups.

> From the issuing of the decree to restore and rebuild Jerusalem until the Anointed One, the ruler, comes, there will be seven "sevens" [49 years], and sixty-two "sevens" [434 years]. . . . After the sixty-two "sevens," the Anointed One will be cut off and will have nothing. The people of the ruler who will come will destroy the city and the sanctuary. The end will come like a flood: war will continue until the end, and desolations have been decreed (9:25-26).

Several elements in this passage are strikingly clear: We're dealing with a definite period of time. That period is subdivided into three groups. The seventy "sevens" have a definite starting point. And, the first 483 years culminate with the appearance of the Anointed One, Israel's long-awaited Messiah.

The "decree to restore Jerusalem" was issued to Ezra the Scribe by Artaxerxes in 458 B.C. The first seven "sevens" bring us to 409 B.C., when Nehemiah and Ezra completed the task of walling and populating the city. The next group of 62 "sevens" brings us to A.D. 26, and the "anointing of the most holy" conducted by John the Baptist when he baptized our Lord Jesus in the Jordan River.

But what about the rest of the prophecy? What about the last grouping of seven years, which are ordained to "put an end to sin," and "bring in everlasting righteousness?"

Time Untold

In an earlier chapter we saw that one feature of Old Testament prophecy is its imprecision in regard to time and sequence. We saw by comparing Isaiah 61 and Luke 4 that both comings of Jesus were referred to in a single Old Testament verse, with no pause, and no way beforehand to separate events associated with Jesus' first coming from events associated with His second. Here, however, there are clues which suggest a time gap exists.

The clues are found in verse 26. Something will happen "after the sixty-two 'sevens'" that is not included in the seventieth seven. What happens is that "the Anointed One will be cut off and will have nothing." Israel's Messiah, destined to bring into being God's righteous kingdom and to rule over it forever, will be cut off with nothing some time after the end of the sixty-ninth and before the beginning of the seventieth week.

The gap between the sixty-ninth and the seventieth "seven" has stretched out now for nearly two thousand years. And we have no way of knowing just when the prophetic clock will begin to tick again and the final seven years of the history of this world will begin.

When *can* those final years begin their flow? At any time. When will they begin again? No one knows!

Tomorrow Today

Daniel's preview of history was intended to comfort Israel through their centuries-long wait. Israel would know no true freedom as the painful decades slowly passed. Pagan peoples would oppress them. Arrogant pagan rulers would try to wean Jewish children from the ways of the Law and would try to force God's people to worship idols and images of Gentile kings. Under these pressures, rebellions would come, only to be crushed as women and children as well as Israeli men paid the penalty for freedom's hot desire.

But Israel was to wait.

The people of God could rest assured. God's Messiah, the Anointed One, would surely come. The Righteous Ruler would appear. And so each generation must find its solace in God and with quiet faith wait for God's promises to be fulfilled.

In view of Daniel's careful explanation of the time that stretched out for people of his day until Messiah would come, it's significant that Daniel, alone among the prophets, makes a clear reference to resurrection. Generations of Jews would die before Messiah came. The ancient promises to Abraham about the Promised Land, the promises to David concerning an unending kingdom, would surely come true. But not for them. Only in resurrection would those who lived and died before Daniel's promised day arrived find hope for themselves, rather than for their children and grandchildren. Daniel 12:1-3 looks at the time of the end and offers words to bring each individual a personal hope.

> At that time your people—everyone whose name is found written in the book—will be delivered. Multitudes who sleep in the dust of the earth will awake: some to everlasting life, others to shame and everlasting contempt. Those who are wise will shine like the brightness of the heavens, and those who lead many to righteousness, like the stars for ever and ever.

And so Daniel's message to the people of his day, and to generations that followed them, was "Not yet!" Not yet—but surely in God's own time. And if that time was not to be within their lifetime, then surely when resurrection came, they too would share in all the good things God has in store for His children.

For Our Today Too?

Today you and I live in the time gap that stretches, undefined, between Jesus' crucifixion (the Messiah's "cutting off" or execution, as in Leviticus 7:20; Psalm 37:9; Proverbs 2:22) and Jesus' glorious return. We too are called to a life of quiet waiting, even though we wait expectantly, realizing Jesus could come today or in some still-distant tomorrow. And as we wait, we too are entrapped in a pagan world, a dark and evil society. Like Israel of old, we are called to wait and as we wait to commit ourselves to live godly, righteous lives. The things that you and I might hope for in this world may never be ours, any more than the freedom for which Israel yearned during the centuries of pagan domination was theirs. But for us too, resurrection lies ahead. When God's good times come, we will share in them, for we will awake to everlasting life.

Explore

1. What difficulties might God's Old Testament people have avoided if they had been ready to wait for God's time for freedom?

2. Why do you suppose Daniel provides Israel with such a specific time frame and picture of the course of history, and yet leaves us without either? How would it make you feel to know the date of Jesus' return? How might it affect your actions if that return were next year? If it were still hundreds of years ahead?

3. Daniel 12:3 speaks of the "wise" (the morally upright, who choose godly paths) and of those who "lead many to righteousness" shining like the stars for ever and ever. What do you think this verse might suggest about how God's people are to spend their time of waiting for Messiah to appear?

CHAPTER SEVEN

Watch!

J ESUS left the temple, trailed by His disciples and the usual crowd. Gesturing to indicate the beautiful buildings so recently expanded by Herod the Great, Jesus remarked, "I tell you the truth, not one stone here will be left on another; every one will be thrown down" (Matt. 24:2).

Later, after a whispered consultation, the Twelve found Jesus alone and questioned Him. "When will this happen, and what will be the sign of Your coming and of the end of the age?" (Matt. 24:3)

These questions launched Jesus into a private teaching session about prophecy, teaching meant for the ears of His followers only and not for the crowd. We have that teaching recorded for us by Matthew, in chapters 24 and 25 of the first Gospel.

Jesus takes the questions in reverse order and, after responding to two, spends most of His time dealing with the third. But Jesus does not answer one of the questions they actually asked. Instead Jesus answers the question they should have asked, but failed to!

The Three Questions
What is the sign of the end of the age? In simple but compelling words, recorded in Matt. 24:4-25, Jesus answered His followers. The years between their time and the end of the age would be filled with wars and rumors of wars. Famines and earthquakes would shake the earth, and nations rise and fall. Persecution and hatred would pursue many of Jesus' followers; false prophets would arise to deceive and distort revealed truth. There would be no end to man's wickedness, no lessening of the human passion for evil. But none of this would mark the end of the age. That mark was already recorded in the prophecy of Daniel concerning the end times, the last "seven" of his seventy sevens of years.

In our last chapter we left Daniel's prophecy without looking at his detailed examination of the events linked with that final seven-year period, which is to begin some time after Messiah, the Anointed One, is cut off.

In Daniel 11 and 12 the prophet tells of wars that will rage over the Holy Land. He speaks of a ruler who will violate a treaty made with Israel, whose armed forces halt the daily sacrifice offered in the Jerusalem temple to set up in the holy place an "abomination that causes desolation" (11:31). The beginning of the seven last, terrible years is uncertain, but "from the time that the daily sacrifice is abolished and the abomination that causes desolation is set up, there will be 1,290 days," or 3 ½ years on the Jewish lunar calendar (12:11).

Jesus identifies this event as the one clear and unmistakable mark of the end of this age. All the terrors of our world's wars and natural disasters pale before what awaits humanity "when you see standing in the holy place 'the abomination that causes desolation,' spoken of through the Prophet Daniel" (Matt. 24:15). "How dreadful it will be in those days," Jesus went on. "For then there will be great distress, unequaled from the beginning of the world until now—and never to be equaled again" (24:19, 21). The awesome period of great tribulation spoken of in nearly all the Old Testament prophets will come then, and none living will escape its terrors. Only because God graciously elects to shorten the days set aside for this judgment will any living survive (24:22).

This "sign of the end of the age" lies ahead of us, how far we do not know. What we have is Jesus' answer to His disciples' question. Only if we are here to witness this awful event will we be *sure* how much time humanity has left to exist on this earth.

What is the sign of Jesus' return? The second question the disciples asked was about Jesus' return. What event or events will signal that?

Jesus speaks plainly about this too (Matt. 24:24-34). Jesus warns that false Christs will appear and that religious rumors will sweep society. But believers are not to rely on such rumors. "For as the lightning comes from the east and flashes to the west, so will be the coming of the Son of man" (24:27).

Jesus' coming will be as sudden and unexpected as the lightning's flash; His sudden presence will be like the fiery bolt that lights up a dark sky. The "sign of the Son of man" which will appear in the sky will be the Son of man Himself, "coming on the clouds of the sky, with power and great glory" (24:30). There will be no sign but Jesus Himself, radiant in glory, commanding at last the unwilling attention of humankind.

What will be the time of Jesus' return? Jesus has given clear answers to two of the disciples' questions. He gives as clear an answer to the third. "No one knows about that day or hour, not even the angels in heaven, nor the Son, but only the Father" (24:36).

God will answer no questions about the time.

Jesus will come—when He comes.

Jesus will appear, shrouded in clouds, to call His own up to join Him in resurrection (1 Thes. 4). He will burst through the clouds "with power and great glory," to send angels to gather His elect (Matt. 24:30-31). Are these two descriptions of the same event? Or are they separate events, each associated with the Second Coming, but to take place at different times during the prophesied seven years? No one knows. What we do know is that the timing is God's secret: we cannot know the *when*, nor can we deduce it.

It is exactly this point that Jesus chooses to expand on. For Matthew goes on to report Jesus' extended answer to the question that His disciples *should have asked* rather than the question they did ask.

What was that question? The question they should have asked was not, "When will this happen?" but rather "What do You want us to do until You return?"

Three Parables

Jesus shares nearly three times as much in answer to the unasked question as He did in answering the three questions His disciples did ask. That emphasis suggests something very important. The certainty of Jesus' return someday should shape the way we live life now. Knowledge of events still future can transform our own todays!

WATCH!

Jesus told three parables intended to define just how expectation of His return is to guide us in our present.

The faithful and wise servant (Matt. 24:45-51). Jesus asks us to imagine a servant who is put in charge of his fellows when their master goes on a trip. It is this servant's responsibility to feed and care for his fellow servants. "It will be good for that servant whose master finds him doing so when he returns," Jesus says. That servant will be given added responsibility and power.

But the servant who thinks, "My master is staying away a long time" and begins to mistreat his fellow servants will be surprised, and judged, when the master appears "on a day when he does not expect him and at an hour he is not aware of" (24:50).

While Jesus is away, He continues to be concerned for the people who are both His servants and His prized personal possessions. How wonderful to realize that you and I can do our Lord's work by showing His love and concern for others in their need. Let's not be like the foolish servant who begins to think his master will never return and uses his position to exploit others for personal gain. Jesus *is* coming again. We who expect Him daily, and as a result pay attention to those things that are His concerns, will be ready when He comes. Those whose expectations of the Second Coming flag will shift the focus of their lives from Christ to worldly gain. And when Jesus comes, all that seemed gain to them will be loss.

The ten waiting virgins (25:1-13). Jesus then told the story of ten virgins, waiting to meet the party of a bridegroom and escort him to the home of his bride. The ten all had lamps. But only five had prepared to wait as long as necessary by bringing extra oil.

But the bridegroom took a long time coming—much longer

than anyone had expected. When the crier shouted out that the bridegroom at last approached, each of the ten had fallen asleep.

They awoke with a jolt and trimmed the carbon from the bits of flax that served as wicks, floating on the olive oil in their flat, open lamps. It was then that five of the virgins realized they were nearly out of oil and begged more from the five who were prepared. The five with oil refused: "There may not be enough for both us and you. Instead, go to those who sell oil and buy some for yourselves."

While they were hurrying to get more, the bridegroom arrived. They were too late! When they finally came back, they found the wedding party inside and the doors closed.

Certainly Jesus' return has been delayed now far longer than any of His disciples could possibly have imagined. We have no way of knowing how much longer still our Bridegroom may delay. What we do know is that each of us, individually, must prepare ourselves for Christ's return. No one else can provide oil for our lamps. It's not a parent's faithfulness or a spouse's love or the commitment of others in our church that will count with Jesus when He comes.

No, Jesus meant what He said when He spoke to each of us alike: "Keep watch, because you do not know the day or the hour." Each one of us must prepare himself or herself, alone, for Christ's return. We cannot prepare for others. And no one else can prepare for you or me.

The talents to be put to use (Matt. 25:14-30). It's one of Scripture's most familiar stories. Jesus told of a man who entrusted his property to his servants while he himself went away. The "talent" Jesus refers to is a large sum of money, well over a thousand dollars, with many times that amount of purchasing power in biblical times. Each servant was given a share of his master's wealth according to his ability. And then the master left on his journey.

While the master was gone, one servant, who had received five talents, "went at once and put his money to work." He gained five more. Another servant, who received two talents, also doubled that amount. But a third, who had been given only one talent, dug a hole in the ground and hid his master's wealth.

It was "after a long time" that the master returned. When he did, he called his servants to give an account of their steward-ship. When the servants who had used their talents well reported to him, each received the same commendation. "Well done, good and faithful servant! You have been faithful with a few things; I will put you in charge of many things. Come and share your master's happiness!" (25:21, 23)

And then the third servant appeared. He confessed fear of his master and told how he had hidden his talent so nothing could be lost. But instead of commendation, that servant faced his master's anger. At the least "you should have put my money on deposit with the bankers, so that when I returned I would have received it back with interest."

As we look through these stories, we note several recurring themes. Together these themes bring the message of each illustration into clear focus, and teach us what it means for us to "watch" as we wait for Jesus to return.

1. The central figure in each story is away, each for a "long time." The waiting stretches out, until many forget that their master may return at any time.

2. Those who wait are given tasks to perform for an absent master. Waiting is not a time for inactivity, but for service.

3. Those who wait make personal decisions during the time of extended delay. Some commit themselves to their service; others exploit or out of laziness fail to use the resources they have been given.

4. When the central figure does return, those who wait must each give an account of their behavior. For those who have watched for the return, and have served faithfully, there is commendation and reward. For those who failed to watch, and turned aside from service, there is the grim warning of punishment and loss.

Jesus' instructions conclude with one final story, not about the waiting years while He would be away, but about that time "when the Son of man comes in His glory" (25:31-46). There is reason to believe that the Judgment Day He describes is not the judgment of Christians, but a judgment on the peoples of the earth (*ethnos*, which means "nations") that have survived the Tribulation time (see 24:32) and uniquely demonstrated their budding faith.

What is so suggestive is what Jesus, now the glorified King of kings, says to the group that stands to His right. He welcomes them into His kingdom, and says, "I was hungry and you gave Me something to eat, I was thirsty and you gave Me something to drink, I was a stranger and you invited Me in, I needed clothes and you clothed Me, I was sick and you looked after Me, I was in prison and you came to visit Me" (24:35-36).

Stunned, this group humbly objects: When did they see Him in such need? And the King replies, "I tell you the truth, whatever you did for one of the least of these brothers of Mine, you did for Me" (24:40).

WATCH!

What an insight into the heart of our God! And what a guideline for you and me as we wait eagerly for Jesus to return. He is not with us now. But the hungry are. The thirsty are. The stranger, the needy, the sick, and the imprisoned are all among us today. And we can serve these, the least in our society, and by such simple ministries demonstrate our faith in our loving Lord.

Explore
1. Why do you suppose the disciples were so concerned about the issues on which they questioned Jesus? Are these valid questions to ask or not? Why?

2. Jesus shifted His followers' attention from "When will You come?" to "What are we to do while we wait?" Why do you think Jesus did this? Try to think of several different reasons.

3. Select one of the three stories Jesus told and study it carefully (Matt. 24:45-51; 25:1-13; 25:14-30). What can you apply to your own life from the story you picked?

4. Look over the four themes the author sees in each of Jesus' stories. Which theme do you believe is most important for you personally? How has awareness of that theme affected your life up to this point?

CHAPTER EIGHT

Hold to the Teachings

W HEN we see the emphasis given to prophecy in the Old Testament and remember the questions Jesus' disciples asked, it's not surprising to discover that early Christians were fascinated by prophecy too—or to discover that, like us, Christians in the first century were confused about times and sequences and current events.

In fact, it was a misunderstanding of prophecy at Thessalonica that prompted Paul to write his second letter to the members of that young congregation.

The church at Thessalonica was established by Paul and Silas on a brief, troubled visit (see Acts 17:1-9). Paul's letters to this church are among the earliest of our New Testament epistles. And it's clear from reading the Thessalonian letters that Paul's instruction of the new believers there included a course on prophecy! It's also clear that Paul's teaching was rooted in the Old Testament prophets and in the words of

Jesus Himself. Yet these new Christians were confused and upset when rumors flew and when contemporary "prophets" suggested that the "Day of the Lord" had already come, and Jesus Christ was about to, or already had, appeared.

So Paul wrote to the Thessalonians about "that day," which has such an important place in the Old Testament's predictive passages, and about an individual we call the "Antichrist."

That Day, the Day of the Lord

The *Expository Dictionary of Bible Words* (Zondervan, 1985) gives us this definition of these important terms.

The phrases "the day of the Lord" and "that day" occur often in the prophets. These are theologically significant phrases; they usually (but not always) identify events that take place at history's end (Isa. 7:18-25). The key to understanding the phrases is to note that they always identify a span of time during which God personally intervenes in history, directly or indirectly, to accomplish some specific aspect of His plan.

What events are most often linked by Old Testament prophets to "that day" and "the day of the Lord"?

Briefly, the day of the Lord is seen as a day of terror, during which Israel would be invaded and purged with an awful destruction. Amos warned those of his day who hoped God would intervene soon: "Woe to you who long for the day of the Lord! Why do you long for the day of the Lord? That day will be darkness and not light" (Amos 5:18). Zephaniah adds, "The great day of the Lord is near—near and coming quickly. Listen! The cry on the day of the Lord will be bitter, the shouting of the warrior will be there. That day will be a day of wrath, a day of distress and anguish, a day of trouble and ruin, a day of darkness and gloom, a day of clouds and blackness" (1:14-15). The dark terror of divine judgment was to be poured out on unbelieving Israel (Isa. 22: Jer. 30:1-17; Joel 1–2; Amos 5; Zeph. 1) and on the unbelieving peoples of the world (Ezek. 38–39; Zech. 14).

But judgment is not the only aspect of that day. When God intervenes in history, He will also deliver the remnant of Israel, bring about a national conversion, forgive sins, and restore His people to the land promised Abraham (Isa. 10:27; Jer. 30:19-31; Micah 4; Zech. 13).

And what will be the outcome of the day of the Lord? "The arrogance of man will be brought low and the pride of men humbled; the Lord alone will be exalted in that day" (Isa. 2:17) (p. 211).

The "Day of the Lord" then is a technical theological term in the Old Testament, that focuses attention on what God will do at history's end. The meaning established in the Old Testament is carried over into our New Testament. In Jesus' teaching, and in the teaching of the New Testament letters, Old Testament prophecy provides the framework within which the future is to be viewed.

So Paul begins his second letter to the Thessalonians with a portrait of God's intervention at history's end, an intervention to take place when Jesus returns. Paul says to those who are persecuted now that God "will pay back trouble to those who trouble you and give relief to you who are troubled, and to us as well. This will happen when the Lord Jesus is revealed from heaven in blazing fire with His powerful angels. He will punish those who do not know God and do not obey the Gospel of our Lord Jesus. They will be punished with everlasting destruction and shut out from the presence of the Lord and from the majesty of His power on the day He comes to be glorified in His holy people and to be marveled at among all those who have believed" (2 Thes. 1:6-10).

Divine judgment will be executed by Jesus when He returns, at history's end, during the great and terrible Day of the Lord.

Already Come?

Now that Paul turns to deal specifically with the notion that "the Day of the Lord has already come" (2 Thes. 2:2), he sets aside for the moment the obvious fact that Jesus has not yet been "revealed from heaven in blazing fire with His powerful angels." After all, the "Day of the Lord" incorporates *all* the events linked in prophecy with history's end. So, setting aside the culminating, visible intervention of Jesus, Paul reminds the Thessalonians of what he has taught them about the *beginning* of "that day."

Don't let anyone deceive you in any way, for that day will not come until the rebellion occurs and the man of lawlessness is revealed, the man doomed to destruction. He opposes and exalts himself over everything that is called God or is worshiped, and even sets himself up in God's temple, proclaiming himself to be God. Don't you remember that when I was with you I used to tell you these things? And now you know what is holding him back, so that he may be revealed at the proper time. For the secret power of lawlessness is

82

already at work; but the one who now holds it back will continue to do so till He is taken out of the way. And then the lawless one will be revealed, whom the Lord Jesus will overthrow with the breath of His mouth and destroy by the splendor of His coming. The coming of the lawless one will be in accordance with the work of Satan displayed in all kinds of counterfeit miracles, signs and wonders, and in every sort of evil that deceives those who are perishing (2 Thes. 2:2-10).

It's clear from the description of the acts of this "man of lawlessness," or "man of sin," that he is the very person referred to in Daniel's prophecy about an "abomination that causes desolation" (Dan. 11:31-32), and the very person indicated by Jesus as the sign of the end of the age (see Matt. 24:15).

The "Day of the Lord," the time of history's end, which will culminate in Jesus' visible return to establish God's rule, "will not come until the rebellion occurs and the man of lawlessness is revealed" (2 Thes. 2:3). But sometime, in the years or decades that lie ahead of us, a great rebellion will be led by a Satan-empowered individual who "opposes and exalts himself over everything that is called God or is worshiped, and even sets himself up in God's temple, proclaiming himself to be God" (2 Thes. 2:4). When he appears we will know that at last the end is at hand and Jesus will soon be revealed to all as Lord and God.

Until then, we cannot know when. But we can know, "Not yet!" We can resist becoming unsettled or alarmed by any prophecy or report that the Day of the Lord has already come (2:2). That day has not come yet. But come it surely will.

The Secret Power of Lawlessness

The New Testament consistently speaks of a specific lawless individual who will be revealed at history's end. But it also speaks of a "secret power of lawlessness" which is "already at work" (2 Thes. 2:7). John calls the individual the "Antichrist," and says, "As you have heard that the Antichrist is coming, even now many antichrists have come" (1 John 2:18). While we await God's timing of the events to take place at history's end, you and I must confront the very powers and principles that will be fully unleashed then.

So what does the New Testament tell us about the spirit of antichrist which is abroad at this moment?

First, the spirit of lawlessness is opposed to "everything that is called God or is worshiped" (2 Thes. 2:4). There's an arrogance, an exaltation of self or of humanity beyond the rightful place of a creature subject to the Creator. The secret power of lawlessness finds expression in the passion of human beings to do what *they* want to do, not what God wants, to selfishly serve themselves, not the Lord.

Second, there is a power in lawlessness. Satan, who will energize the Antichrist and enable him to perform "all kinds of counterfeit miracles, signs and wonders" which deceive those who are perishing, ensures a counterfeit "success" to his followers today. They may well have health, position, power, wealth, or other benefits and ascribe to false beliefs or distorted values.

Third, those moved by the spirit of antichrist deny that Jesus is the Christ. Any claim to relationship with God or boast of spiritual sensitivity that involves a denial "that Jesus Christ has come in the flesh" is of the Antichrist (1 John 2:22; 4:2-3). The teachings of such a person represent the spirit of falsehood and not the Spirit of God (4:6).

84

But how does the spirit and secret power of lawlessness express itself today? How do we recognize its influence? There are so many, many ways! We see it in the cloak of morality thrown over evil as a disguise. Christians who oppose the killing of the unborn are angrily charged with intolerance, or worse. Believers who take a stand with Scripture against such practices as homosexuality are victims of public vilification, like one well-known figure who recently lost a television job in Atlanta. Individuals who espouse this "alternate lifestyle" are paraded on TV and quoted in a press that supports their demands not only for "rights," but also that those who object to their sin be silenced. Television rating races provoke multiplying series that feature promiscuity. Evil persons are given sympathetic treatment in TV and movie scripts, but Christian ministers are cast as fools, criminally greedy, or at best insensitive and cold.

Oh yes—the spirit of antichrist is at work in our society. It opposes everything that is of God, offering counterfeit objects of faith and commitment, denying that Jesus the Son of God has come in the flesh, to live and die as a human being, and in His death to redeem all who believe from their bondage to sin.

The Antichrist, that individual who plays such a critical role in the future prophesied by Old Testament and New Testament alike, will surely appear. But even now you and I need to be aware of the secret power that will energize that individual and be alert for expressions of the spirit of antichrist in our contemporary world.

Tomorrow Today
There are many questions about time and sequence raised by what Old Testament and New Testament say of the

85

Antichrist, the man of lawlessness. Does he appear at the beginning or in the middle of Daniel's final "seven" of years? Does Jesus' coming to destroy him at the end of that time imply that Christians will live through the great Tribulation of those days? Or will Jesus come for us before the final drama unfolds, before Christ appears visibly to all at history's end?

These are the kinds of questions that the Bible does not answer specifically, any more than Jesus would answer the disciples when they begged to know, When?

But there are questions the Bible *does* answer, questions like, "What does this insight into God's certain tomorrow mean for us today?" According to Paul and to John, here are some of the implications for today of the vision of the Antichrist to come.

First, let's not become unsettled or alarmed by prophetic systems that look to current events and insist "Now! He's coming now!" We are not to let anyone deceive us in any way, "for that day [the time of God's final, direct, personal intervention in history] will not come until the rebellion occurs and the man of lawlessness is revealed" (2 Thes. 2:3). If you are looking for signs of Jesus' coming, there is only one event that will announce, *the time is now!*

Second, we are to recognize that the secret power of lawlessness, which will be fully unveiled in the Antichrist, is at work today in our own society. The full expression of that evil influence is restrained now. Many believe that "the one who now holds it back" (2 Thes. 2:7) is the Holy Spirit, resident now in Jesus' church. Even so, that evil influence is all around us, and the spirit of antichrist pervades our society.

In view of this terrible reality, Paul exhorts those who have been saved through belief in the truth about Jesus to "stand firm and hold to the teachings we passed on to you" (2 Thes.

2:15). In a society flooded with deceitful values and counterfeit faiths, we Christians must be both steadfast and wise. We
must measure every claim, examine every morality, question
every implied value. And we must measure them by the
teachings of the Word of God. When we are sure that we
know what God's Word establishes as right and good and
true, then we must take our stand, and stand firm.

And Paul adds this word: God loved us. By His grace He
gave us eternal encouragement and good hope. We can trust
God to encourage our hearts and to strengthen us "in every
good deed and word" (2 Thes. 2:16-17).

John makes this same point. The Spirit of God within will
enable us to recognize the Truth (1 John 2:26-27). We must
"test the spirits to see whether they are from God" (4:1) and
must reject everything that originates in the spirit of antichrist. Because God in us is greater than that spirit of evil that
is in the world, we *will* recognize truth. By God's Spirit and
His grace, you and I will overcome.

Explore

1. What are some ways you can think of in which the
spirit of antichrist is at work in our society? What popular
moral values would you identify as antichristian? What popular religious beliefs? How do you think the spirit of antichrist
may be expressed in modern entertainment media?

2. The author notes that the Christian's response to teaching
about the Antichrist involves becoming sensitive to the hidden
power and spirit of antichrist in the contemporary world.
Specifically, we are to distinguish the true from the false by
study of the Scripture, and then "stand firm and hold to the

teachings" of God's Word.

What do you suppose "standing firm" and "holding to the teachings" involves? What do you suppose it does *not* mean?

Can you list ways in which you can "stand firm" against some particular expression of the spirit of antichrist?

CHAPTER NINE
Sons of Light

PAUL writes passionately, as always, as he exhorts his Thessalonian flock on "how to live in order to please God" (1 Thes. 4:1). He urges these young believers to live in holiness and with a deep, brotherly love and insists they take an honest, hardworking approach to daily life and win the respect of outsiders. Then, he introduces an unexpected prophetic note.

Brothers, we do not want you to be ignorant about those who fall asleep [die], or to grieve like the rest of men, who have no hope. We believe that Jesus died and rose again and so we believe that God will bring with Jesus those who have fallen asleep in Him. According to the Lord's own word, we tell you that we who are still alive, who are left till the coming of the Lord, will certainly not precede those who have fallen asleep. For the Lord Himself will come down from heaven, with a loud command, with the voice of the archangel and with the trumpet call of God, and the dead in Christ will rise first. After that, we who are still alive and are left will be caught up with them in the clouds to meet the Lord in the air. And so we will be with the Lord forever. Therefore encourage each other with these words (1 Thes. 4:13-18).

The Rapture Question?

This passage in 1 Thessalonians is one of the most familiar and at the same time most controversial of the Bible's glimpses into the future. It describes what we've come to call the Rapture, that moment when Jesus' own are caught up to meet Him at His return, to be with our Lord forever. The passage is often read at funerals, for it promises a grand reunion with our loved ones. Those who have died "in Christ," united to Him by a personal faith, will accompany Jesus at His return. Then, in a moment of time, those who have died in Christ experience resurrection. At the same moment we who are living in that day will be transformed. Together, hand in hand with those we've lost, we'll rise to meet Jesus in the clouds. Never again will we be separated—from Jesus or from our loved ones. What an exciting and comforting message! No wonder we Christians, while we grieve at the passing of a loved one, are not crushed like the rest of humankind who live without hope.

We are not strangers to hope! In Jesus, and in the promise of His coming, we have the promise of certain joy.

But the "Rapture question" is not about *what* will happen then. The question, like so many raised by modern students of prophecy, has to do with *when.* Will the event pictured here take place before the Tribulation described by Daniel and by

Jesus and by Paul? Will it happen sometime during that last "seven" of years? Or will it happen at the end of that terrible time? I can't begin to guess how many books have been written debating this point. But I know I've read at least a dozen and have seen many more I haven't touched.

That's often been the problem with our study of prophecy. We're more concerned with how to fit an event into our system or our prophetic scheme than we are with the Scripture's purpose in introducing a particular prophetic theme.

Certainly here Paul doesn't discuss systems. He doesn't link the Rapture to Daniel's abomination of desolation. He doesn't say whether or not Jesus discussed the same event or another in Matthew 24:31. Paul simply teaches us that Jesus *is* coming. When Jesus comes, the believing dead will rise again, united with the living, and together we will join our Lord in glory.

But with this picture of what lies ahead for us tomorrow, Paul explains the impact the Rapture is to have on our Christian lives today! Yes, there's comfort when our loved ones die. But it has another vital impact as well.

Jesus Is Coming

There are a number of references in the New Testament to the return of Jesus. And there are three very special Greek words associated with His return. When we understand these words we have a better grasp of what Christ's return will mean and of the impact expecting Jesus should have on our lives.

Jesus is coming to be present with us. One of the Greek words associated with the Second Coming is *parousia.* The word means "presence" or simply "coming," but emphasizes both the idea of "being there" and the idea of "having come."

When *parousia* is used to describe the return of Jesus, it directs our attention to the fact that Christ will return in person and that His being with us will have special meaning for us then.

Parousia is found four times in Matthew 24 (vv. 3, 27, 37, 39), which emphasizes the sudden, unexpected, and devastating impact of His return on those who do not believe. As we have seen, the emphasis in Matthew 24–25 is on the fact that until Jesus *is* here, we are to watch and faithfully serve our absent Lord.

First Thessalonians speaks of Jesus' coming as a *parousia* three times. When Jesus is present, Paul will see his dear converts standing before his Lord (2:19), and he yearns for them to be holy in that presence (3:13). In our Rapture passage, Paul again emphasizes Jesus' personal presence: only His being here can initiate our final transformation.

In 2 Thessalonians Paul explains that Jesus will not appear in person until the Antichrist has been identified (2:3-12). Then, by the "splendor of His coming," the splendor of His personally being here, Jesus will destroy this one whom Satan has energized. Peter joins John in urging us to live close to the Lord now so that "when He appears we may be confident and unashamed before Him at His *parousia*" (1 John 2:28; cf. 2 Peter 3:11-13).

Parousia, then, is a word for Jesus' coming that (1) emphasizes the fact that Christ is coming in person to be with us, and (2) focuses our attention on what His return will mean for us who believe. We will be transformed at Jesus' coming, to share the glory of His resurrection and to share His joy in a world at last set right.

Jesus is coming to interrupt history. The word *epiphaneia* simply means "appearing" or "appearance." A religious term in Greek culture, *epiphaneia* suggested a visible manifestation of a hidden deity. In the New Testament this term focuses our attention on the fact that when Jesus' presence is revealed, it will be with a starburst of power, burning the image of our Lord into the retinas of a faithless, spiritually blind humanity. Our "blessed hope" is focused on the day when Jesus' glory will be seen by all (Titus 2:13).

Paul combines *epiphaneia* and *parousia* in an exciting way in 2 Thessalonians 2:8. There Paul writes of the Antichrist, whom Jesus will overthrow "by the splendor [epiphaneia—flaming, visible manifestation of power] of His coming [parousia—personal presence]." The presence of Jesus, which means comfort and joy to you and me, means the violent overthrow of evil.

We who believe recognize the splendor cloaked by the manger and by the cross. But when Jesus comes again, it will be in unshrouded, unmistakable power. And God has reserved a crown for those who love His appearing, looking eagerly beyond the illusory pleasures of this world to visualize a coming that will shatter forever the empty dreams of a lost humanity (2 Tim. 4:8).

Epiphaneia, then, emphasizes that Jesus' return will constitute a disrupting intervention in a world hardened to God's grace. Then the world we know will be replaced by Jesus' righteous kingdom, and He will reign in beauty. To love His appearing, to yearn for His return in its character as *epiphaneia*, means to reject the values of this world and build our lives on the holy and on the pure—to be dissatisfied with today and yearn for the holy and pure destined to dominate in that day.

Jesus is coming to unveil reality. The third Greek word associated with the Second Coming is *apokalypsis*. It means "to disclose or bring to light." In the Bible this word is used of the disclosure of truths that could not have been discovered by us unaided, but have been shared with us by God. When linked with the Second Coming, this word highlights the fact that, although true information from God has been provided in the Bible, Jesus Himself is the One who will be disclosed on His return. Then all previous revelation about Him will be confirmed, as Christ's coming serves as God's final, culminating disclosure of reality.

Luke 17:22-35 portrays the shock of that day as Jesus is suddenly revealed. Humanity, caught unaware, will know the devastation of the divine judgment as Jesus is revealed in blazing fire with His powerful angels to punish and destroy (2 Thes. 1:7-8).

Apokalypsis stresses the following facts: Jesus' return will be witnessed by all, His glory undeniable. Jesus' return initiates the Day of Judgment on unbelievers, and the fulfillment of the believers' hopes. Significantly, Jesus' return as an *apokalypsis* means the full vindication of the Gospel, as all that has been expressed in Scripture and denied by humankind is shown to be real after all.

Our Tomorrow, Our Today

First Thessalonians 4:13-18 gives us a glimpse of what Jesus' second coming will mean for you and me. Jesus will be personally present in that wonderful *parousia,* and in His bright presence we believers will be lifted up and transformed.

But the return of Jesus means different things to different groups. For those who love His Coming as an *epiphaneia,* Jesus' return will shatter the world in which they

94

felt so uncomfortable, so unfulfilled. For those who love this world, Jesus' return will shatter all their hopes and dreams, for this world and its desires which have been twisted by sin must be set right. For those who have rejected the Gospel and ridiculed revelation, Jesus' return means judgment and facing the reality from which they so hastily fled.

Yes, Jesus will come again. And every passage that explores His coming has a special message for you and me. That message has nothing to do with how this or that event fits in our prophetic systems. That message is simply this: "Jesus is coming" is a word we must hear, and heed, now!

Let's look back in 1 Thessalonians 4 and see how Paul develops that word we must hear and where he shows us how to heed it, now.

Paul begins in 4:1-12 by urging his readers to live to please God. "It is God's will," he says, "that you should be holy; that you should avoid sexual immorality; that each of you should learn to control his own body in a way that is holy and honorable" (4:3). He goes on to speak of brotherly love and exhorts his readers in verses 11 and 12 to make it their ambition "to lead a quiet life, to mind your own business and to work with your hands, just as we told you, so that your daily life may win the respect of outsiders and so that you will not be dependent on anybody."

And then, after sharing his bright vision of the Rapture that lies ahead, Paul returns to application. "About times and dates we do not need to write you, for you know very well that the Day of the Lord will come like a thief in the night" (5:1-2). Jesus will come—unexpectedly. The unsaved will not be ready when Jesus comes. "But you, brothers, are not in darkness so that this day should surprise you like a thief. You are all sons of the light and sons of the

95

day. We do not belong to the night or to the darkness. So then, let us not be like others, who are asleep, but let us be alert and self-controlled" (5:4-5).

See it?

You and I are not like others, for we look forward to Jesus' return, knowing that it will mean resurrection for our loved ones and endless life for you and me! The promise of the Rapture and our happy expectation of Jesus' *parousia* underline the fact that we do *not* belong to the darkness. We belong to the day, for our destiny is intertwined forever with that of God's Son!

So, "since we belong to the day, let us be self-controlled, putting on faith and love as a breastplate, and the hope of salvation as a helmet" (5:8).

It is our hope—our confident expectation in the salvation Jesus will soon bring to us—that keeps us alert and self-controlled. When we look ahead expectantly, realizing that through His death Jesus has destined us for salvation rather than wrath, we bond together with one another and seek to encourage and build one another up for a living faith and an increasingly holy life.

Explore

1. What are some of the implications of Jesus' coming for non-Christians? For disobedient Christians? For committed Christians? What are the implications for you?

2. Read through 1 Thessalonians 4 and 5 and underline each phrase that suggests how Paul says his vision of the Rapture tomorrow should affect the believer's today. Which of the

applications seems most important for modern Christians?
Why?

CHAPTER TEN

With a Roar

PETER is sure as he pens his second letter that he will soon put his earthly body aside, "as the Lord Jesus has made clear to me" (2 Peter 1:14). In a sense this brief letter contains the great apostle's last, dying words.

One little book I've noticed in bookstores and the library is a book entitled *Famous Last Words*. They range from the supposed last whisper of a Roman emperor who tried to stamp out Christianity ("Thou hast conquered, O pale Galilean") to the deathbed advice of an American financier ("Buy low, sell high"). But the point, of course, is that last words are supposed to reveal an individual's most deep-seated and important concerns.

What then was Peter's deepest concern? He wrote to remind us of truths in which we are already established, truths that help us go on in a life of godliness (2 Peter 1:3-8).

Burning with this desire, the aging Peter does not look back to remind his readers of all that God has done. Instead he looks ahead and outlines what God will do, sure that knowledge of the future best prepares us to live successfully in perilous times.

The Prophetic Word

Peter begins with a reminder to his first-century readers. He has shared things about Jesus' "power and coming" which he himself witnessed (2 Peter 1:16). Peter refers here to what he saw on the Mount of Transfiguration, when Jesus' "face shone like the sun, and His clothes became as white as the light" (Matt. 17:2). Peter knows from personal experience the glory to be revealed at the Second Coming!

But Peter goes on. We also "have the word of the prophets made more certain" (2 Peter 1:19). The record of fulfilled prophecy reinforces our conviction "that no prophecy of Scripture came about by the prophet's own interpretation. For prophecy never had its origin in the will of man, but men spoke from God as they were carried along by the Holy Spirit" (1:20-21).

The prophets too speak of the coming glory and underline the significance of what Peter is about to say. We are to "pay attention to" the prophets' word, for it is "a light shining in a dark place, until the day dawns and the morning star rises in your hearts" (1:19).

False Teachers

Peter's second chapter contains a warning against false teachers who will arise "among you." There are several descriptions given in Scripture that help us recognize false teachers and false prophets, those who claim to convey God's message but who are not sent by Him. These indicators are carefully detailed in both testaments. How do we recognize false teachers?

	Jeremiah	2 Peter	Jude
● Doctrinal Indicators			
destructive heresies,			
denying the Lord	23:13	2:11	
● Personality Indicators			
bold, arrogant	23:10	2:10	16
despise authority		2:10	8
follow corrupt desires	23:14	2:10	4, 19
of sinful nature			
love monetary profit		2:15	12
● Ministry Indicators			
appeal to "lustful desire			
of human nature	23:14	2:18	16
promise "freedom"			
to the depraved	23:18-19		

Both the teaching and the moral life of the false teacher are corrupt, and while such persons promise their followers freedom, they themselves are slaves of their own depravity (2 Peter 2:19). But we Christians "have escaped the corruption of the world by knowing our Lord and Saviour Jesus Christ" (2:20). How terrible if we were to turn our backs on righteousness to become "entangled" by following false teachers in the passions and ways of a lost world (2:20-21).

It is in the context of this danger that Peter asks us to "recall the words spoken in the past by the holy prophets and the command given by our Lord and Saviour through your apostles" (3:2). Then, to stimulate wholesome thinking, Peter asks us to consider one feature that has been taught by prophet and apostle alike—the end of the world!

The Material Universe

Our Judeo-Christian heritage features a unique view of the material universe. While modern evolutionists, like the ancient Greek philosophers, suppose that the physical universe is the starting point for an understanding of reality, the Bible takes a completely different position. The universe did not come first, and life did not emerge from some chance combination of random atoms bombarded by cosmic rays. First of all there was God. It is in God we find the origin of all things.

In fact, the material universe is totally dependent on God. It sprang into being only at His spoken word (Gen. 1). It exists now only because it is held together by Christ's divine power (Col. 1:17). The universe was not even created for its own sake. The vast heavens and our spinning earth were shaped to be the home of humankind, the stage on which the drama of sin and redemption could be played out. Far from being the starting point, the material universe can only be understood when its subordinate position is understood.

What's more, this universe is a temporary thing. It's not the mountains and the seas of planet earth that are eternal; the personality of each fragile human being will outlast them all. Each individual, self-conscious and aware, will exist throughout eternity to come, but the Bible speaks plainly of an end of our world. "Behold, " Isaiah reports, "I will create a new heavens and a new earth. The former things will not be remembered, nor will they come to mind" (Isa. 65:17).

Our present universe will be replaced, for God has said "lift up your eyes to the heavens, look at the earth beneath; the heavens will vanish like smoke, the earth will wear out like a garment and its habitants die like flies. But my salvation will last forever, my righteousness will never fail" (Isa. 51:6).

So we can't look to the material universe to search out our origins in its past. Nor can we find the meaning of human existence in the hope of further evolution in the future. The material universe is but a stage, and when the final curtain on life's drama falls, the stage will be torn down, and a new stage quickly erected on which the actors, who alone remain, can take their new and better parts in God's bright eternity.

A New Attitude

Remembering these teachings of the prophets and of Jesus Himself, Peter asks us to analyze our own attitudes toward this world and to be alert to the empty arguments of false teachers. Let's trace Peter's argument as he looks ahead with us in chapter three of his second letter.

Scoffers will come (3:3-9). These last days are filled with scoffers who ridicule the notion that God will intrude in history and who follow their own evil desires. They'll lightly dismiss warnings of the judgment to come and base their belief on a simple but fascinating argument. "Where," they will say, "is this 'coming' He promised? Ever since our fathers died, everything goes on as it has since the beginning of Creation" (3:4).

This argument is a keystone of modern scientific thinking. Modern geology and modern evolutionary theory both rest on this assumption. In "uniformitarian" geology it is the belief that every feature of the earth, from mountain peaks to the deepest chasms in the sea, can be explained by natural processes that we can observe now. In evolution it is the notion that higher forms of life must have developed by natural processes from the less complex. Each system is rooted in the conviction that "everything goes on as it has from the begin-

103

ning of Creation." Neither allows for intervention by God. God, if God exists, is some "merely" spiritual being locked out of the material universe by immutable natural law. Jesus *can't* come, they say, because everything that goes on in the world is subject to the laws of nature that have controlled our universe since time began.

Peter has two answers. First, "they deliberately forget" that the world was formed at God's Word. He, as Maker, is superior to the material universe He created. They forget too that God has demonstrated His sovereignty and *has* intervened! The world of long ago was "deluged and destroyed" by the waters of the Genesis Flood. God *has* intervened! He showed both great power and His firm commitment to judge sin, when He destroyed the civilization that once existed on this earth in a cataclysmic scourging of earth's surface by its waters (Gen. 6–8). By word of this same God "the present heavens and earth are reserved for fire, being kept for the day of judgment and destruction of ungodly men" (3:7).

So Peter totally rejects uniformitarian thought. The physical universe has never been independent. It has always been subject to the Word of God. God's past intervention to judge a sinning society gives us warning that God will surely intervene again.

But the scoffers also ridicule God's delay. "Where is this 'coming' He promised?" Today, nearly 2,000 years have passed since Jesus promised to return. No wonder some, noting that the apostles themselves expected their Lord soon, feel the delay disproves the promise. If Jesus were to come, He would have come before now.

Peter has an answer to this objection too. "Do not forget this one thing, dear friends: With the Lord a day is like a thousand years, and a thousand years are like a day. The Lord is not slow in keeping His promise, as some understand slowness. He is patient with you, not wanting anyone to perish, but everyone to come to repentance" (3:8-9). Jesus late? Why, to God it's as though only two brief days have passed since Christ arose from the grave! God does not measure time as we do.

But there's another vital thought here. Any delay has been a gift. Our patient God is providing individuals with the opportunity to repent. God does not want any to perish. So until Jesus does come, grace reigns.

But when Jesus comes, then it will be too late!

The Day of the Lord (3:10-14). We learned in an earlier chapter that the "Day of the Lord" is one of the Bible's technical theological terms, used to indicate a time when God intervenes personally in the course of history. It is usually linked with judgment and typically focuses our attention on history's end. Peter uses "Day of the Lord" in this way here as he reveals more about one of those awesome events biblical prophecy foretells.

> The Day of the Lord will come like a thief. The heavens will disappear with a roar; the elements will be destroyed by fire, and the earth and everything in it will be laid bare. . . . That day will bring about the destruction of the heavens by fire, and the elements will melt in the heat. But in keeping with His promise we are looking forward to a new heaven and a new earth, the home of righteousness" (3:10, 12-13).

This world and everything in it will disappear with a roar in a furnace of fire that will outshine the sun, as the core of our earth is laid bare and the very elements of which it is composed explode. The most terrible hydrogen bomb is nothing compared to the awesome moment when God will dispose of our material universe, emptying space in preparation for the formation of His promised new heavens and new earth.

With this vision burning into our minds, Peter confronts us with a purifying thought. "Since everything will be destroyed in this way, what kind of people ought you to be?" (3:11)

False teachers and false prophets appeal to the lustful desire of sinful human nature and so lead people into the very lifestyle that marks out this world for judgment (2:18). Those they deceive become entangled again in the world and its corruption (2:20). *As long as our hopes are focused on what can be ours in this world, we are vulnerable to being led astray!* As long as we lust for this world's wealth, for this world's position, for this world's success, we are vulnerable to the temptations that lead the rest of humankind into sin.

So Peter wants us to burn one vision of the future into our hearts. He urges us to gaze ahead with the prophets and to realize that the whole material universe is destined for destruction. Nothing here can satisfy! Nothing here can last!

In view of that, what manner of people ought we to be? "You ought to live holy and godly lives as you look forward to the day of God and speed its coming" (3:11-12). You ought to look forward to the new heavens and earth, the home of righteousness. And "since you are looking forward to this, make every effort to be found spotless, blameless, and at peace with Him (3:14).

Tomorrow Today

Peter does not deal with times or sequences. He writes about the end of the world because he is so intensely concerned for the believers of his, and our, today. Peter knows that if our hopes and expectations are focused on the material world, we are vulnerable to moral corruption. Peter knows too that if our hopes are fixed on Jesus' return, because we know that this world and all that is in it is doomed, we will be on our guard. If our hearts yearn for God's new and righteous world to come, we will be on our guard, and we will "make every effort to be found spotless, blameless, and at peace with Him."

Explore

1. How many of the wrong choices people make are made to gain something that can have value only in this world? Would they make the same choices if they were convinced the world and everything in it might be gone tomorrow?

2. How does looking forward "to a new heaven and a new earth, the home of righteousness," stimulate us to "live holy and godly lives"? (3:11, 13)

3. Think of your possessions in this world. Are there any for which you would sin if you thought you would lose them otherwise? Are there any things you want badly enough that you would be tempted to sin in order to obtain them? In what way could this prophetic word of Peter's help guard and protect *you*?

CHAPTER ELEVEN
Splendor Ahead

I T is awe inspiring to look ahead. We can easily be caught up in prophecy's visions of the world-shaking events that surely will take place on planet earth.

We see a final conflict, with plagues that threaten all humanity. Does Revelation suggest atomic war, with raging famine and disease caused by radioactive dust? We don't know. We see the unification of the western world under a leader who will become the Antichrist. Have the foundations for his political union been laid in our day? Is the evil leader alive now? We don't know. A time of terrible tribulation is coming. In our lifetime? We don't know. Soon Jesus will come to catch up believers into the clouds. When? We don't know. The material universe in which we live will flame out of existence, its very atoms torn apart. When? We can't be sure. But how fascinating to guess, to try to fit the glimpses of the future given us in Scripture together. How fascinating to ponder what will happen to humankind.

I sense two problems with this admittedly fascinating approach to prophecy. The first has already been discussed. When Scripture shares its glimpses of what lies ahead, the Bible's emphasis is not on tomorrow but on today. God shows us aspects of the future, yes. But His purpose is to help us live godly lives now. We've seen it in the lives of the Old Testament prophets, like Amos and Habakkuk and Jeremiah. And we've seen it in the apocalyptic teaching of Jesus in Matthew 24–25, in visions of the Antichrist, of the Rapture, and finally in Peter's portrait of the end of the world. In each case the Bible's own emphasis rests squarely on how what lies ahead should shape our perspective now and motivate us to lead godly lives.

When we study prophecy in order to develop a systematic view of what's ahead, we have missed the "today" purpose God had in mind in revealing various aspects of the future through His servants the prophets.

The other problem with prophetic studies that major on outlining the future is that we may become so caught up in the big picture that we lose sight of God's concern for the individual.

This world, with its burden of history past and of history to come, will disappear one day. The events that fascinate us "will not be remembered, nor will they come to mind" (Isa. 65:17). What really counts—what counts because it is the *only* lasting thing in the universe—is individual human beings. Each of us, each man and woman, each child, will continue to exist, self-conscious and aware throughout eternity.

We can study the world-shaking events still to come. But let's remember that there is also prophecy concerning the future of individuals. It's to this personal prophetic word, that directly affects you and me, we turn now.

Resurrection Ahead

Paul says it simply. "If only for this life we have hope in Christ, we are to be pitied more than all men" (1 Cor. 15:19). You and I have turned away from what the world offers and chosen holiness in the conviction that there is more to life than earth's brief, bitter years. But our choice of holiness, our battle against temptations, our self-giving rather than selfish taking, make sense only if God is real and if life persists beyond the grave.

In 1 Corinthians 15 the apostle does look beyond. His teaching here is prophecy that's uniquely for you and me. Paul doesn't talk about what is ahead for the world, but what is ahead for the individual who has faith in Jesus.

Teaching on resurrection isn't limited to the New Testament. True, the Old Testament does emphasize what will happen to God's covenant people, Israel. But individuals are not forgotten, as many passages allude to personal resurrection (cf. Gen. 5:22-24; Deut. 32:39; 2 Kings 2:11-12; Ps. 16:9-11). Other passages are even more explicit. God will set death aside (Isa. 25:8), and "your dead will live; their bodies will rise. You who dwell in the dust, wake up and shout for joy" (Isa. 26:19).

Daniel's teaching is the most clear. "Multitudes who sleep in the dust of the earth will awake: some to everlasting life, others to shame and everlasting contempt" (12:2). Death isn't the end. Every individual will awake.

When we turn to the New Testament, we're gripped by a growing excitement. The individual resurrection hinted at in the Old Testament is in clear focus of the New Testament.

What may be most exciting of all is God's unveiling of what resurrection will mean to you and me. We are destined "to be conformed to the likeness of His [God's] Son" (Rom. 8:29).

When Jesus returns and our resurrection takes place, we who are now the children of God "shall be like Him, for we shall see Him as He is" (1 John 3:2). That inner pull toward sin that we fight against now will be gone then, as resurrection purifies us fully from every trace of sin. In the resurrection we will shine with a holiness that is like God's own.

The Apostle John describes our destiny in words he hears announced from God's throne and which are recorded in Revelation.

> Now the dwelling of God is with men, and He will live with them. They will be His people and God Himself will be with them and be their God. He will wipe every tear from their eyes. There will be no more death or mourning or crying or pain, for the old order of things has passed away (Rev. 21:3-4).

When that day dawns, there will be no more curse. We will see God's face, and we will reign for ever and ever (Rev. 22:3).

Jesus' Resurrection and Ours

The Bible's most extensive teaching on resurrection is found in 1 Corinthians 15. Let's follow Paul's reasoning as he reassures those in Corinth who were confused about this personal prophetic theme.

Jesus' resurrection has already taken place (1 Cor. 15:1-11). Paul first reviews the evidence that Jesus Himself experienced a literal, physical resurrection from the dead. The earliest preaching of the Gospel emphasized Jesus' resurrection, along with the offer of forgiveness of sins (cf. Acts 2:24-32; 3:14-16, 26; 5:30; 7:55; 10:39-43). In these verses Paul notes evidence for that resurrection. If we combine what he reports with other passages, we can see that the resurrection of Christ is one of the best attested of ancient historical events. All the apostles saw and talked with the resurrected Lord, as did many other individuals named in Scripture. In chronological order these are Mary of Magdala (John 20:11-18); several women (Matt. 28:8-10); Peter (Luke 24:34); two on the Emmaus road (Luke 24:13-32); a group on the day of the resurrection (John 20:19); Thomas (John 20:24-30); disciples on the seashore (John 21); over 500 gathered followers (1 Cor. 15:6); James (1 Cor. 15:7), and others at the Ascension (Acts 1:1-9). With so many eyewitnesses alive during the years the New Testament was written, there is no possibility that the resurrection story could be a fraud.

Jesus' resurrection guarantees our own (1 Cor. 15:12-34). In Paul's time some of those who were part of the Corinthian church insisted that there would be "no resurrection of the dead" (15:12). Paul responds. In that case "not even Christ has been raised. And if Christ has not been raised, our preaching is useless and so is your faith" (15:13-14). Christianity is *about* resurrection. Christianity is about a world beyond our own. God's promise that we will be resurrected and gain a place in the world to come is central to our faith.

What's more, Jesus' resurrection *guarantees* our own. Jesus "was declared with power to be the Son of God by His resurrection from the dead" (Rom. 1:4). It is as the all-powerful Son of God that Jesus Christ offers us salvation and promises us a resurrection patterned on His own.

Paul looks ahead and links our individual destiny with the unalterable purpose of our God. Resurrection comes to "each in his own turn: Christ, the firstfruits; then, when He comes, those who belong to Him. Then the end will come, when He hands over the kingdom to God the Father after He has

113

destroyed all dominion, authority, and power" (15:23-24).

The reference in 15:29 to being baptized for the dead is to a practice some of the Corinthians had adopted. Paul is not teaching that this *should* take place; he is simply observing that the Corinthian's own practice assumes a resurrection. For if life ends with physical death, what value could there possibly be in being baptized for someone who is forever gone? Yes, Adam's sin brought death—but Christ's sacrifice brings us eternal, resurrected life.

Jesus' resurrection body is the pattern for our own (1 Cor. 15:35-56). Paul then responds to those who are curious about what resurrection will be like. "How are the dead raised? With what kind of body will they come? (15:35) The answers aren't complete and do not really satisfy our curiosity. It's likely that human language simply lacks the concepts and words to adequately convey what we will be. But what there is is exciting.

Paul notes simply that our resurrection body will correspond with our present body, but will be infused with power—it will be spiritual rather than natural. Because it bears the "likeness of the Man from heaven" (15:49), the resurrection body will be imperishable, glorious, vital, and endlessly alive.

Because in our resurrection we will bear Christ's likeness, some have suggested that Jesus' resurrection body sets the pattern for our own. His body was "flesh and bones" (Luke 24:39). Is this in contrast to flesh and blood because "the life of a creature is in the blood" (Lev. 17:11), and a resurrected person is infused with a different order of life? And what are the capacities of that order of life? Jesus appeared among His disciples in a locked room (John 20:26). Was it teleportation? Or did the resurrected Jesus simply move between the atoms

114

of our material universe?

Whatever our future resurrection involves, we know that the limitations of our physical nature will be gone. The perishable will become imperishable, weakness will become power, immortality will replace mortality, and holiness will burn out every trace of latent sin.

Resurrection for All?

One of the dark themes in God's revelation of the future is linked to resurrection. Every individual will be raised and will exist forever, self-conscious and aware—but not everyone will be transformed.

Daniel said it. Some will awake "to everlasting life, others to shame and everlasting contempt" (Dan. 12:2). Jesus Himself spoke more often about hell than He did about heaven! And Revelation, the New Testament's great apocalyptic book, gives us this grim description.

> I saw the dead, great and small, standing before the throne, and books were opened. Another book was opened, which is the Book of Life. The dead were judged according to what they had done as recorded in the books. The sea gave up the dead that were in it, and death and Hades gave up the dead that were in them, and each person was judged according to what he had done. Then death and Hades were thrown into the lake of fire. The lake of fire is the second death. If anyone's name was not found written in the Book of Life, he was thrown into the lake of fire (Rev. 20:12-15).

To be judged according to what we have done means condemnation, for we have all sinned and fallen short of the glory of God (Rom. 3:23). How vital then that you and I have our names written in the Book of Life through personal faith in our Lord Jesus Christ, who died for us to make our forgiveness and our resurrection sure.

Tomorrow Today

How does Scripture apply prophecy about the transforming resurrection ahead for believers?

In 1 Corinthians 15 Paul concludes his teaching on resurrection this way: "Therefore, my dear brothers, stand firm. Let nothing move you. Always give yourselves fully to the work of the Lord, because you know that your labor in the Lord is not in vain" (15:58).

You and I know our destiny.

You and I know our identity.

We are God's own children even now, and when Jesus returns, our transformation into His moral likeness will be completed. We are not like those who will perish with this world, infected forever with the sin that has corrupted human desires. Knowing who we are and who we will be, we find added strength to stand firm. Nothing on this earth can move us, and we give ourselves to the work of the Lord knowing that nothing we do for Him will be in vain.

Explore

1. Can you picture yourself in your resurrection? How will you be different? What will remain the same?

2. The certainty of resurrection—to endless life or to certain shame—should motivate us to reexamine our personal rela-

tionship with Jesus. Have you trusted yourself fully to Him?

3. John prophesies that when Jesus returns, we who are God's children will be transformed and actually be like Him (1 John 3:2). John goes on to say "everyone who has this hope in him purifies himself, just as He [Jesus] is pure" (3:3).

What do you think it means to have this hope in us? What do you think it does *not* mean? To what extent have you found that 1 John 3:3 is true in your own life?

CHAPTER TWELVE
God's Tomorrows, Our Todays

AS we've explored the "real" meaning of prophecy, we've only sampled the prophetic themes and passages of Scripture. Rather than try to examine all the themes or link together events the Bible describes in a systematic way, we've looked at typical Old Testament and New Testament prophecies to see how God intended such information about the future to affect the lives of the prophet's or the apostle's contemporaries. And we've tried to see how the same information is intended by God to affect our lives, providing guidance or perspective on life in our own today.

One of the purposes of this study has been to let Scripture's prophetic words touch you—and touch me. Whenever we come to the Word of God, we come reverently, listening to hear what the Lord has to say to us personally.

But there was another purpose. That purpose was to help you learn a way of studying prophetic passages on your own—a way of looking at prophetic passages so that you'll see how to discover more than just images of tomorrow.

In this final chapter, as a kind of final "exam" on how to study Bible prophecy for personal growth and enrichment, I will provide background information on two more prophetic passages—and let *you* study them to discover for yourself what God's tomorrows mean for your own todays.

The New Covenant

Jeremiah, the "weeping prophet," suffered with Israel at a time when generations of disobedience finally culminated in divine judgment. He knew only too well that Israel and Judah had failed again and again to respond to the Lord. God had given Israel His Law through Moses, but that Law had consistently been disregarded or violated. Even the revivals that flared briefly under several of Judah's godly kings had failed to halt the slide of God's people into idolatry, injustice, and immorality. The warnings of prophets like Amos and of Jeremiah himself had been ridiculed. God's spokesmen were persecuted and at times even killed.

Jeremiah has been given God's promise that His people's exile from the promised land will be temporary. He's even been told the length of time involved: seventy years.

But Jeremiah might well have remained despondent. The Law of God, and even God's earlier discipline, had failed to produce righteousness. God's people kept on turning away from Him, no matter what blessings or punishments God brought upon them. Israel and Judah might well return to the land—but would anything *really* be different? Wouldn't they simply slide back into the sins and tragedies of the past?

There was another terrible thought that must have passed

through the mind of the godly few in Jeremiah's time. Did the destruction of Jerusalem and the temple where God had promised to put His name mean that God had finally deserted His people? Had their sin finally been so great that God could no longer bear with them? Was this national disaster something like the Genesis Flood—the sweeping away of society so that God could begin again, start afresh?

It is against the background of these two dominating concerns that Jeremiah is given his prophetic vision of a New Covenant which will be made with the house of Israel. This covenant is specifically "not like" the earlier Mosaic Covenant—an external Law—that governed the nation and its people.

> "This is the covenant I will make with the house of Israel after that time," declares the Lord. "I will put My law in their minds and write it on their hearts. I will be their God, and they will be My people. No longer will a man teach his neighbor, or a man his brother, saying 'Know the Lord,' because they will all know Me, from the least of them to the greatest," declares the Lord. "For I will forgive their wickedness and will remember their sins no more" (Jer. 31:33-34).

What's more, Jeremiah goes on to make it plain that the ancient covenant promises to Abraham and to David will be kept (see 33:19-26). Despite Judah's and Israel's sin, and despite the terrible judgment each experiences, the Lord declares that the days are coming "when I will fulfill the gracious promise I made to the house of Israel and to the house of Judah." And that day is identified as the days and the time of the Messiah (33:14-18).

We see many echoes of this New Covenant prophecy in our

New Testament. When Nicodemus came to Jesus by night, this teacher of Israel was surprised that Jesus spoke of being "born again." There should have been no surprise. Jeremiah foretold a time when God's Law, written on cold stone, would be infused in the human heart and mind. The new heart and the new birth are one and the same; a teacher of the Old Testament like Nicodemus should have known.

We hear Jeremiah's words echo as Jesus broke the bread and shared the wine, announcing to His disciples that these represented the blood of the New Covenant, shed for them. We hear Jeremiah's words echo in Paul's teaching that we "are being transformed into His likeness with ever-increasing glory" (2 Cor. 3:18) by the Spirit of God. And we hear them as the writer of Hebrews repeats the ancient promise of a New Covenant and then tells us that that covenant's benefits are ours now through the sacrifice of Jesus Christ (Heb. 8:10-13; 9:15).

Against this background we can study Jeremiah and sense how the tomorrow he describes was vital knowledge for Judah in their today.

A Future for Israel?

One of the most important theological issues linked with prophecy concerns Israel. Did the Christian church displace the Jewish people in God's plan? Are the Old Testament prophecies about a national existence and a national glory for Israel to be fulfilled in some symbolic way in the blessing of individual Christians or of the body of Christ?

One of the most serious charges the Apostle Paul and others had to face in the first century was that if Christianity were true, then God would be proven a liar. God could not be faithful to His promises to Israel and at the same time set them and the Law aside in favor of a new, different "Christian" people.

In Romans Paul deals with this question on a number of levels. He shows that by-faith salvation is rooted in the Old Testament and is not an invention of Jesus' apostles. He shows us that righteousness could never have come by the Law. And in Romans 9 through 11 Paul deals with the problem of national Israel.

His argument is carefully reasoned and does not become prophecy till chapter 11. Paul begins by showing that not every Jew is a child of promise. Physical descent isn't the criterion. God has historically chosen some, but not all, of Abraham's "natural children" (9:6-13). And of course God, who is sovereign in His universe, is free to do this (9:14-21). In fact, the Old Testament shows that God has always intended to call out His people from Gentile as well as Jewish stock (9:22-29). If the Jewish people are currently set aside, it's not because God was unfair or unfaithful, but because they tried to base their relationship with the Lord on works, not on a by-faith righteousness through trust in Christ (9:30-33).

In Romans 10 Paul makes another important point. God's welcome of Gentiles doesn't mean that He has turned from the Jews! The Gospel message is for Jew and Gentile alike, "for there is no difference between Jew and Gentile—the same Lord is Lord of all and richly blesses all who call on Him, for, 'Everyone who calls on the name of the Lord will be saved' " (10:12). Now, just as in Old Testament times, some but not all of Abraham's descendants are being saved. All who respond to the Gospel, Jew or Gentile, can and will be saved.

But now Paul turns to the critical prophetic question. "Did God reject His people?" (11:1). Paul's "No!" is based on two theses. First, those Jews who have trusted Jesus, and there were and are many, are today "a remnant chosen by grace." Just as in historic judgments on Israel a remnant (some, but not all) were delivered, so today those Jews who believe in Jesus are being saved (11:1-9).

Although the Jewish nation as a national entity has been set aside and the door of salvation opened to all, Paul expects a future acceptance of the nation. It will be like "life from the dead" (11:15). Temporarily broken from a tree so new branches can be grafted in, the original Jewish branches will be grafted back to the trunk (11:11-24).

It's now that Paul himself turns to prophecy, or at least to provide an inspired interpretation of an earlier prophet's words.

> I do not want you to be ignorant of this mystery, brothers, so that you may not be conceited: Israel has experienced a hardening in part until the full number of the Gentiles has come in. And so all Israel will be saved, as it is written: "The deliverer will come from Zion; he will turn godlessness away from Jacob. And this is my covenant with them when I take away their sins." As far as the Gospel is concerned, they are enemies on your account; but as far as election is concerned, they are loved on account of the patriarchs, for God's gifts and His call are irrevocable (11:25-29).

Repeated Prophetic Themes

These are just two more of the many prophetic passages in our Bible. The dominant emphases of the Old Testament are summed up simply in this extended quotation from my *Word Bible Handbook* (Word, 1982), p. 373.

It is . . . clear that the prophets do predict a conclusion to history. The world will not stumble on endlessly, with nothing resolved and no purposes achieved. Instead the prophets sound a note of triumph. History will close with a great culmination. God will act to fulfill the promises made in the covenants. . . . Evil will be dealt with, holiness vindicated, and blessing ushered in. What themes do they return to when looking into the distant future? . . .

(1) *The regathering of Israel.* At history's end God's [Old Testament] people are in their land, regathered there by Him for the final working out of God's purposes (Isa. 11:11-12; 14:1-3; 27:12-13; 43:1-8; 66:20-22; Jer. 16:14-16; 23:3-8; 30:10-11; 31:8, 31-37; Ezek. 11:17-21; 20:33-38; 34:11-16; 39:25-29; Hosea 1:10-11; Joel 3:17-21; Amos 9:11-15; Micah 4:4-7; Zeph. 3:14-20; Zech. 8:4-8).

(2) *World Conflict and Tribulation.* At history's end the nations of the world, under the leadership of a northern power, assemble to invade and crush the people of God. The time is also one of great suffering and tribulation, which comes as a judgment on God's people as well as the people of the world. Yet a remnant survives the great destruction (the nations: Ezek. 38–39; Dan. 11:40; Joel 2:1-17; Isa. 30:31-33; the sufferings: Deut. 4:30-31; Isa. 2:12, 19; 13:6, 9; 24:1, 3, 6, 19-21; 26:20-21; Jer. 30:7; Ezek. 13:5; 30:3; Dan. 9:27; 12:1; Joel 1:15; 2:1-2, 11, 31; 3:14; Amos 5:18-20; Zeph. 1:14-15, 18; Zech. 14:1; the survivors: Isa. 4:3-4; 6:12-13; 26:20; 65:13-14; Jer. 15:11; 33:25-26; Ezek. 14:22; 30:34-38; Hosea

3:5; Amos 9:11-15; Zech. 13:8-9; Mal. 3:16-17).

(3) *The Glorious Kingdom.* The final battle is resolved by God's own intervention, as His Messiah appears. With the power of evil crushed and holiness vindicated, a great spiritual conversion takes place among Jews and Gentiles, and the Messiah, a ruler sprung from David's line, establishes an endless kingdom (Isa. 2:1-4; 4:2-6; 9:6-7; 11:1-13; 24:1-23; 32:1-5; 33:17-24; 35:1-10; 52:7-10; 60:1–61:6; 66:15-23; Jer. 22:1-8; 31:1-27; 33:14-26; Dan. 2:31-45; 7:1-28; 9:20-27; Mal. 3:1-5; 4:1-6; Ezek. 20:33-42; 34:20-31; Hosea 3:4-5; Joel 2:28–3:2; 3:9-21; Amos 9:9-15; Obad. 15-21; Micah 4:1-5; Zech. 2:1-13; 14:1-21.

The New Testament accepts this scheme and expands on it. There is word of a New Creation, of a thousand-year reign by a returned Christ (Rev. 20:1-6), of meeting Christ in the air, of the destruction and replacement of the physical universe, of resurrection, and of judgment. All this will come. But as we wait, we are to learn from prophecy how to live now.

Excitement Ahead

There is joy in studying any portion of God's Word. The God who spoke to men and women centuries ago continues to speak. The Bible is a living, vital Word, and as we read, we recognize God's voice.

The prophets have a special place in the canon of Scripture. Their words have attracted believers across the ages. We are captivated by their bright vision of yet future events and drawn to puzzle over the meaning of the images the prophets paint for us in their powerful words. Even though we can never be certain just how the future they portray will unfold, we do glimpse that future's broad outline. We sense the dynamic movement of history; we are swept up in the certainty that the God who acted in the past to create and redeem maintains a confident grip on whatever it is that lies ahead.

Yet we can easily miss the real meaning of prophecy and the true excitement of studying the prophets. We can become preoccupied with the prophetic systems, trying to sort and fit foretold events into some ordered scheme. While this may not be wrong, it is at best uncertain. Scripture seldom puts prophetic events into sequence, rather, it tends to focus on one particular aspect of God's future work at a time. And as we have seen, Scripture tends to link the meaning of what lies ahead with the present experience of those who first heard the prophetic word.

Here is where we can find the true excitement of studying prophecy and where we can find its most significant meaning. The deepest issues of human life remain unchanged across the ages. As we study the words of the prophets and understand their times, we begin to discover the powerful impact that the prophetic word has had on ordinary men and women. We gain fresh insights into the things that trouble us and gain new direction for the decisions we must make each day. In short, we too hear in the prophetic Word the voice of the living God, speaking not just of tomorrow, but speaking directly of our own todays.

Yes, excitement does lie ahead. There is excitement in studying the prophets of our Old Testament. There is the excitement that comes from meeting God in a fresh, new way and discovering that the God of Amos and Daniel and Habakkuk and of all the rest still speaks through men of old to you and me today.

Explore

1. Choose either of the two prophecies for which the author provides background, and study the one you choose. From your study, how do you believe the prophecy applied to the "today" of the writer's contemporaries? How does it apply to you in your own today?

2. What is the single most important thing you have learned in reading and studying this book? How has that thing affected you or the way you live your life?

Dear Reader:

We would like to know your opinion of *Tomorrow Today*. Your ideas will help us as we strive to continue offering books that will satisfy your needs and interests.

Send your responses to: VICTOR BOOKS
1825 College Avenue
Wheaton, IL 60187

What most influenced your decision to purchase *Tomorrow Today?*
- ☐ Front cover
- ☐ Title
- ☐ Author
- ☐ Back-cover material
- ☐ Price
- ☐ Length
- ☐ Subject
- ☐ Other: _____

What did you like about this book?
- ☐ Helped me understand myself better
- ☐ Helped me understand others better
- ☐ Helped me understand the Bible
- ☐ Helped me understand God
- ☐ It was easy to teach
- ☐ Author
- ☐ Good reference tool

How was this book used?
- ☐ For my personal reading
- ☐ Studied it in a group situation
- ☐ Used it to teach a group
- ☐ As a reference tool
- ☐ For a church or school library

If you used this book to teach a group, did you also use the accompanying leader's guide?   ☐ Yes   ☐ No

Please indicate your level of interest in reading other Victor Books like this one.
- ☐ Very interested
- ☐ Somewhat interested
- ☐ Not very interested
- ☐ Not at all interested

Would you recommend this book to a friend?
- ☐ Yes
- ☐ No

Please indicate your age.
- ☐ Under 18
- ☐ 18-24
- ☐ 25-34
- ☐ 35-44
- ☐ 45-54
- ☐ 55 or over

Would you like to receive more information about Victor Books? If so, please fill in your name and address.

NAME: _____

ADDRESS: _____

_____

Do you have additional comments or suggestions regarding Victor Books?